Natural Dyes

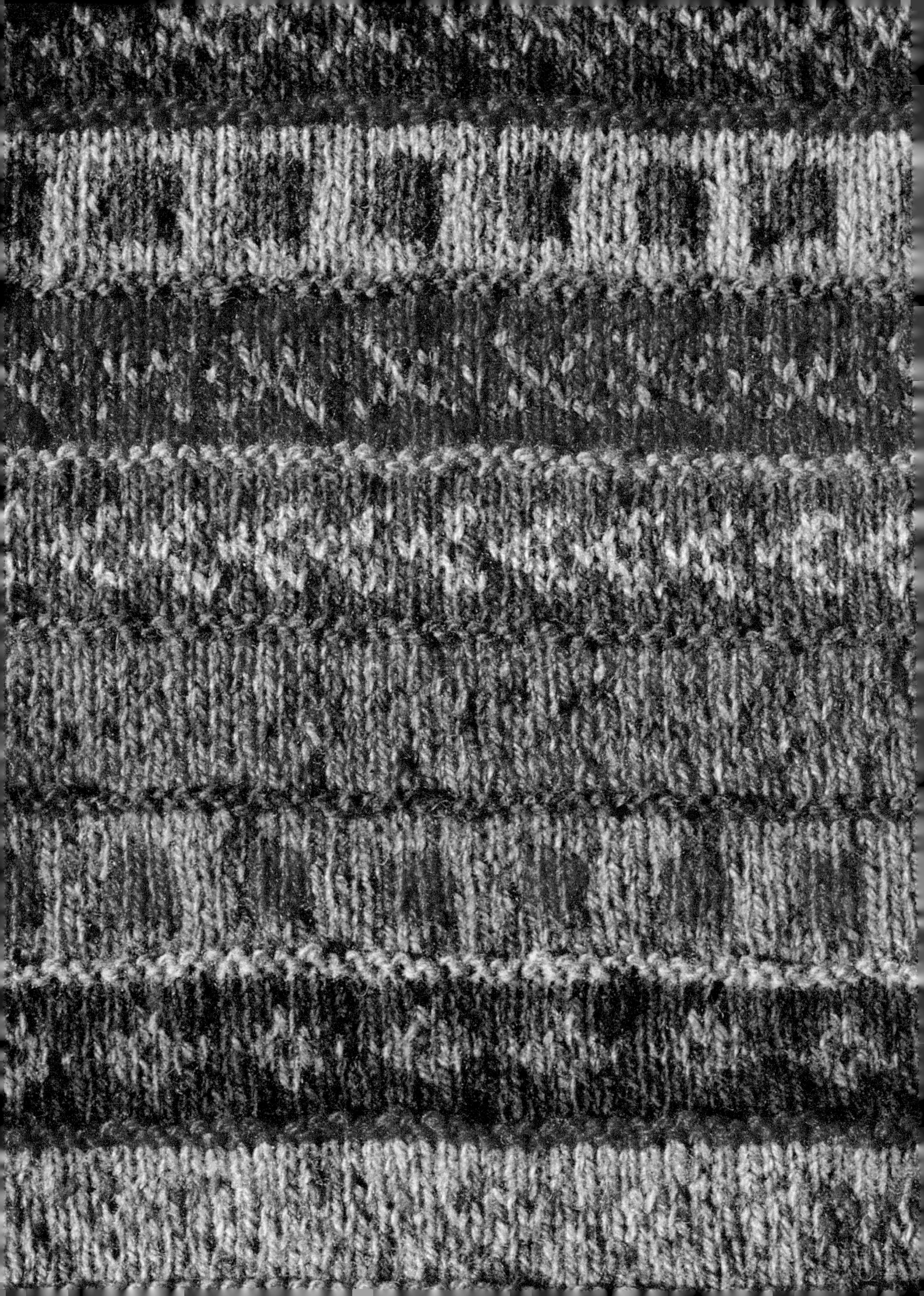

Natural Dyes

Judy Hardman and Sally Pinhey

THE CROWOOD PRESS

First published in 2009 by
The Crowood Press Ltd
Ramsbury, Marlborough
Wiltshire SN8 2HR

www.crowood.com

This impression 2018

British Library Cataloguing-in-Publication Data
A catalogue record for this book is available from the British Library.

ISBN 978 1 84797 100 5

Frontispiece: Knitted waistcoat, using wools dyed with madder, indigo and dyer's
greenweed.

Acknowledgements
I would like to thank Sally Pinhey, firstly for her encouragement to write the book and
secondly for her magnificent botanical paintings and garden designs; my husband
Peter for years of tolerating the concoctions brewed in the kitchen and workshop and
the odd plants grown in the garden – his skill with the computer and camera have been
much appreciated; my daughter Sam, who pointed out my errors with the chemistry
and advised on computer use; Roger Pinhey for the initial proof reading; Gill Read for
invaluable botanical advice; Ruth Whitty for her gardening expertise; Alexandra
McArdle, who has been using natural dyes for years and who has shared with me many
experiments and plants. All the knitted items are mine using mostly the fleece from my
Shetland sheep and the woven items are from my collection.

Disclaimer
The authors and the publisher do not accept responsibility, or liability, in any manner
whatsoever for any error or omission, nor any loss, damage, injury, or adverse outcome
of any kind incurred as a result of the use of the information contained in this book, or
reliance upon it.

Typeset by Servis Filmsetting Ltd, Stockport, Cheshire
Printed and bound in Great Britain by Severn, Gloucester

Contents

Knitted hat using wool dyed with madder, weld and hollyhock.

Introduction

Plants have been grown to add colour to fibre for thousands of years. Many of the plants, which still grow today, have also been used for food, flavourings, perfumes, cosmetics and medicines. The dyers in 3000BC would have known from experience which plants produce colour and about 'mordants', which help the dye 'bite' so that it can be retained by the fibre. Today we might call some of the plants they used weeds because the recipes have never been written down or are lost.

The purpose of this book is to show how plants grown in your garden can be used to give a good range of colours on animal fibres such as wool and silk. Accurate identification of plants is important and the botanical illustrations will help you to do this. The plants have been selected because they are good sources of colour and are easy to grow or are available as 'weeds'. We will take you through the processes, from plant selection to preparation of the fibres to the dyeing, so that you can get a range of vibrant colours. The colour samples of dyed wool have been obtained by using four different mordants; they have been wound on to bobbins in the same order so that it is easy to identify each shade. The intensity of the colour will vary depending not only on how much of the dye plant has been used

Dye plant materials.

Madder Root

Walnut Husk

Onion Skins

Coreopsis Flowers

Yew Bark

Yew Heartwood

Elder Leaves

but also the season, the growing conditions and the variety of the plant, so the colour illustrated can only be a guide.

GROWING PLANTS

You can create a garden that will supply you with a range of plants for dyeing. Advice about growing conditions and the size of plants is included in Chapter 6. Your climate and soils will affect your choice. Some plants are likely to take over but others need careful nurturing. Some plants are classed as weeds, such as nettle, dock and bramble; some are hedging plants, such as elder and privet. Traditional dyes do produce the best and most permanent colour. Plants that will grow in a temperate climate include madder, weld, dyer's greenweed, woad and walnuts.

Specialized seed merchants can supply many of the dye plants. Ordinary nurseries will be able to provide the more common plants. There may be other plants of the same species that will provide the same or similar colours or may have little of the coloured component. It is always interesting to try. For example, madder root contains more alizarin, which gives the red, than lady's bedstraw, yet they are of the same species.

GATHERING PLANTS

The parts of the plant to be used are indicated (*see* Chapter 4 and Appendix 1) and may be the flowers, fruits, leaves, stalks, roots, wood or bark. You need to dye enough for your needs in one batch, as it is difficult to reproduce colours. Most plants can be dried but fresh ones usually produce a brighter colour. Bark and roots need to be boiled longer, soaked, ground up or fermented to extract colour. Many factors will have an effect on the colour, including the growing season, time of year and day, amount of sunshine, amount of water used, type and cleanness of fibre, length of process, and how the fibre is rinsed at the end. The light fastness and wash fastness are important, so plants suggested tend to be the ones that will retain their colour. The colours indicated can only be a guide.

TYPES OF DYE

There are three types of dye – direct, additive and substantive.

Direct Dyes

These are dyes that do not need a mordant. They often give fugitive colours (not 'light fast' and 'wash fast'), and tend to fade away. These dyes include berry juices, safflower petals and walnut husks. Sometimes the addition of mordants will help with the fastness.

Additive Dyes

Additive dyes are those that need a mordant. Mordants are chemicals that enable the dye molecules to adhere to the fibres, and give light and wash fastness. Different mordants will produce different colours in the same dye bath. They tend to be metal salts and some of the traditional ones are poisonous. What you need to do is weigh your dry materials accurately so that all the mordant is taken into the fibre and the bath will contain little residual chemical. Adding cream of tartar, formic acid, acetic acid or oxalic acid assists take-up of the dye and brightens the colour. After mordanting you will need to rinse the fibres to remove any loose mordant that might make the take-up of the dye patchy. It should be noted that chrome mordanted fibre, if made into a garment, may cause an allergic skin reaction in some cases. Sometimes if alum is used, then an 'after-mordant' of copper or chrome might improve fastness and will darken the colour. This means that once the initial dyeing process is completed then the yarn is put into the second mordant bath, brought to simmer in thirty minutes, kept at that temperature for a further thirty minutes then removed and rinsed. You should not dispose of chrome or tin down your domestic drain. A soakaway might be the solution, or evaporate the water and dispose of the residue through a specialized waste disposal company. You are advised to wear rubber gloves when handling the mordants. A face mask is advisable when dealing with fumes from mordanting with chrome, tin and oxalic acid.

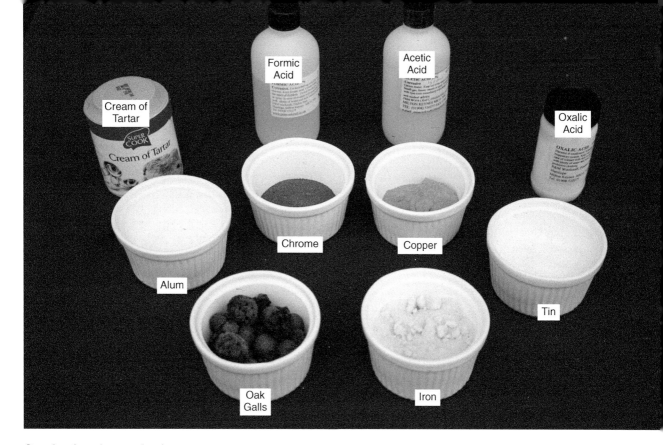

Samples of mordants and assistants.

Substantive Dyes

Substantive dyes are vat dyes: they do not react chemically with the fibre but are deposited on the surface of the fibres. The preparation of the vat dyes requires special care and they work much more quickly than mordant dyes. Indigo and woad are used in vat dyes. If you want to produce green from a combination of yellow and blue, you will need to mordant the wool in order to dye the yellow before you dip into the indigo or woad bath to add the blue colour.

MORDANTS

Alum

Another name for alum is aluminium potassium sulphate. It is the safest mordant, although excess leaves the wool sticky and tends not to be as light fast as other mordants. Cream of tartar (tartaric acid) assists the take-up of alum and improves the take-up of the dye and brightens the colour slightly, reducing the quantity of alum needed.

Chrome

Chrome is used in the form of potassium dichromate. It is sensitive to light, is an irritant to skin, it gives off poisonous fumes, and it is also likely to pollute the environment. Formic acid assists the take-up of chrome and therefore reduces the quantity required. The author no longer uses Chrome.

Copper

In dyeing, this is used in the form of copper sulphate. The combination with dilute acetic acid or white wine vinegar assists the take-up of copper and reduces the amount needed. It tends to 'sadden' (darken) the colour but enhances the greens.

Tin

Tin is used in the form of stannous chloride. It is poisonous and makes the wool harsh and brittle but does brighten the colour, especially the reds, oranges and yellows. Oxalic acid or cream of tartar assists the take-up of tin. Fibres could be pre-mordanted with alum and a very small quantity of tin used to brighten the colour. Like chrome, tin is likely to pollute the environment.

Iron

Iron is used in the form of ferrous sulphate (copperas). It tends to 'sadden' colours; it also hardens the yarn and eventually rots the fibres. Ferrous sulphate can be produced by leaving rusty nails in water for a week but this would be of an unknown dilution and therefore difficult to reproduce. The fibre should not be left in an iron bath for more than thirty minutes. It is commonly used as an after-mordant and many of the greens are produced in this way, adding a very small amount in solution to yellow dye. Black has traditionally been obtained by using iron on pre-dyed browns and oranges.

Oxalic acid

Oxalic acid is poisonous and is contained in rhubarb leaves and sorrel. The rate of use is between 75% and 100% of dry weight of wool. The leaves are simmered for forty-five minutes and the liquid strained off. When simmering, it gives off poisonous fumes so it is best to keep the lid on the dye pot, and a face mask is advisable.

Tannic acid

This is found in oak galls (the growths on the trunk produced by fungi and insects) and oak bark and is used for tanning leather and in mordanting cotton and vegetable fibres.

Glaubers salt

This is a levelling agent and when added to the dye bath before dyeing will help the even take-up of colour, but may make the colours slightly duller.

CHAPTER 1

Equipment and safety precautions

Dye pans

Stainless steel is the ideal material for dye pans, and bowls and buckets are readily available. Unchipped enamel bowls and pans are as good, but if they are chipped the iron beneath the enamel coating will sadden the colour of any dyes used. Aluminium pans have the advantage of having lids, but as aluminium is one of the mordants, it may alter the shades of colour obtained. 'Burco'-type electric boilers are very useful for large quantities. The stainless steel ones have a copper heating element inside the main container which means that you are potentially adding another mordant. If a fine dyestuff is used you may find it sinks through the holes of the protecting tray and will block the heating element. In this case you may find that it burns out the element. There are aluminium 'Burco' boilers; in these the elements are underneath and therefore this problem does not arise.

Heat sources

If you use your kitchen, make sure it is well ventilated and wipe up all dye spills immediately. Portable gas stoves can be used outside but you may need to use a draught protector on the windward side and you need to be careful that the flame does not blow out. The gas bottle must be away from the heat of the stove. Check the rubber hose is well fitting to both the gas bottle regulator and to the stove. If there is a smell of gas, check the fittings, otherwise there could be an explosion.

Dyeing equipment.

Portable electric plates are good but the heat is not as controllable as with gas. Be careful not to let the temperature rise above the recommended one particularly for indigo, woad and madder, otherwise the shade is spoiled.

If you use a wood fire you will need a tripod to suspend the dye pot, otherwise stability may be a problem once the pot is full of water and dye material.

Stirrers and tongs

Stainless steel spoons and rods are good but can get hot. Wooden spoons and dowel do not get hot but do absorb the dye. Glass rods are good, but make sure they are the heatproof variety. Wooden and stainless steel tongs are useful for lifting hanks of yarn.

Thermometer

You will need a thermometer to help maintain temperature limits on such dyes as madder and woad. It needs to have a range from 0–100°C. Keep this thermometer solely for dyeing.

Measuring equipment

Choose weighing scales that measure weights up to 2kg. Metric ones are better than Imperial as it is easier to work out the percentages you need for mordants, dye material and fibre. A scale that weighs accurately from 0–100g is needed for the mordants. A letter balance will weigh low weights.

Measuring jugs for large quantities (up to 1 or 2 litres) are invaluable. Stainless steel and glass jugs are best, but heatproof plastic ones are acceptable if kept clean. For smaller quantities a large syringe or small measuring cylinder can be used. Keep this equipment separate from food preparation equipment.

A kitchen timer helps to remind you when the time is up, although it is rarely critical.

Storage

Make sure a label written with permanent pen states what the liquid is, the chemicals it contains and the date. Glass jars are best; use dark glass for light-sensitive chemicals such as chrome. For larger

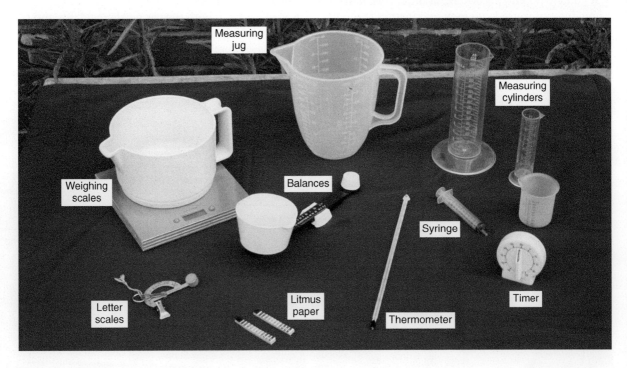

Measuring equipment.

quantities plastic 5l containers are good. If you use drinks containers, be careful to store them out of reach of children. Do not pour boiling liquids into plastic containers, as they have a habit of melting and distorting.

Bowls and buckets

These are always useful, particularly if you have lids for them.

Sieves and colanders

These are useful for draining off dye plant material, so anything from a soil riddle to a fine sieve would be useful. If you leave the dye material in the dye bath when dyeing you may want to place it in a mesh bag. If the material of the bag is coloured be aware that the colour may leak into the solution.

If you leave the dyestuff in with the yarn, be prepared to pick out and shake the bits free. Sometimes this will lead to a patchy take-up of the dye.

Dyestuff that is free to move in the bath with the fibre does give a more consistent shade. If you start both the plant and fibre from cold in the bath, bring the heat up gently to the recommended temperature, then simmer for an hour. Don't be surprised if there does not seem to be a change of colour in the first hour of this process – it takes time for the dye to enter the water.

Rinsing and drying

Once the mordanting or dyeing process is completed you need to squeeze the liquid out. If using very small samples a salad spinner is an efficient method. For larger quantities an electric spinner saves both water and effort and is less likely to cause the wool to felt. Some washing machines have a spin cycle that does not add water; this is preferable because the fibres may felt if bombarded with either very cold or very hot water as the machine is spinning.

Once the rinsing process is completed the yarn can be spread out to dry on a rack or a line. If there are still pieces of dye material adhering then they may well come out at this stage or when the hank is wound into a ball.

If you find the dye colour is coming off on your hands you will need to rinse again; the addition of salt or vinegar to the final rinse often solves this problem.

SAFETY PRECAUTIONS

There are several hazards that you should be aware of when dyeing, and for which you need to take suitable precautions.

Chemical inhalation

The mordants chrome, copper and tin are especially hazardous chemicals. A face mask should be worn when using these mordants as the powder if inhaled can cause burns and damage to the mucous membrane and when in solution can give off toxic fumes. A mask is particularly essential if you are prone to breathing problems. Rubber gloves should also be worn when weighing out. Close windows so that the powders cannot blow about, and pour slowly.

An electric spin dryer can be useful for larger quantities of wool.

Dissolving mordants

It is advisable to pour the powder or crystals into a small container, add a small quantity of water and make a paste using a stainless steel teaspoon, then add to the main bath. Thoroughly wash whatever containers you use for weighing and mixing. Dispose of the packaging safely.

Irritation to skin

Some dye plants have juices that may cause irritation. When you are dyeing, the colour is as likely to attach to your skin as well as to the fibre, so continue to wear rubber gloves and use stirrers and tongs to move dyestuff and yarn about in the dye pot.

Eye irritation

For contact lens wearers there is the additional hazard of the dry powders irritating the eyes.

Damage to clothing

An apron will protect your clothes and, if waterproof, will catch the inevitable drips. You may decide that you will keep a set of clothes that you use only when you are dyeing.

Damage to surfaces

Protect surfaces on which you place the dye pots. Use a good waterproof surface or cover with newspaper or thick plastic sheet. If using portable stoves, something that is heatproof would be better.

Spillage of liquids

Have a mop or sturdy floor cloth to hand to clear up any spillage of liquid as soon as possible to reduce the chance of slipping and staining.

Ventilation

A well-ventilated dye area is important: there are many dye plants that have penetrating smells and some of the processes give off fumes.

Hot dye pots

Oven gloves or insulated clothes are useful when handling hot dye pots, particularly if pouring boiling liquids. Make sure the dye pot is stable when full. Wait until the liquid is cool before trying to drain off the liquor. Use a funnel or colander that is large enough to contain the plant material. If it overflows when boiling, it can easily pour over feet and make a mess of the floor surface.

Miscellaneous precautions

Containers for dyestuffs must be clearly labelled with what they are and the date.

Chrome will need to be kept away from light, preferably in a dark glass container with a screw top, out of reach of children and pets.

Instructions must be read carefully before starting; have everything you need close by.

Acids should be added to the water (*not* the water to the acid). For spillages have a supply of clean cool water on hand to flush eyes and skin if they are splashed with acid. Baking soda neutralizes any remaining acid.

Alkalis such as caustic soda: flush with affected part with water and neutralize the alkali with some very dilute vinegar.

Disposal of waste: the remains of mordant bath should not be put down the sink, it is best tipped into a soakaway in an area not used by children and pets. If you weigh the mordant and yarn accurately there should be very little of the mordant and its assistant (the chemical added to improve the take-up of the mordant) left in the solution. Do not be tempted to add more than the recommended amount of mordant.

Septic tank: do not tip any dye solution into a septic tank. If you test the pH then you can neutralize the remaining liquid: if it is too acid, add caustic soda; if it is too alkali, add vinegar.

Removal of residues: if you let the dye bath stand, any solids will sink and then a cloth should be used to remove any dye left around the dye pan, and disposed of. The vegetable residue of the dyes may be composted.

Children and pets must be closely supervised at all times.

CHAPTER 2

Preparation for dyeing and dyeing techniques

PREPARING FIBRES SUITABLE FOR DYEING

Most animal fibres will take dye. Wool and silk are the most straightforward; cotton and vegetable fibres are more complicated. We will be giving recipes for all of these fibres.

Raw fleece

Raw fleece can be dyed, but you may want to use the dye liquor (the liquid remaining after the

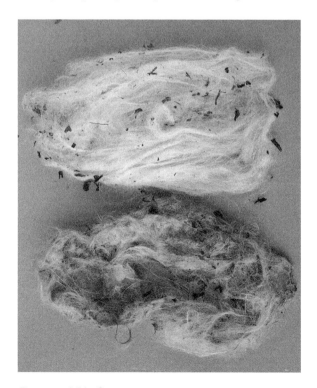

Dye material in fleece.

vegetable dyestuff has been boiled for an hour and then removed). This is because the vegetation is often difficult to separate from the fibres even by carding. Putting the fibre in a nylon mesh bag is another solution but this means that the dye liquor does not circulate well. Carded fleece can be treated in the same way.

Spun yarn

This should be wound in hanks and tied in at least four places with loose figure of eight or double figure of eight cotton or wool ties. This should not be done tightly or the dye will not penetrate. It is easier to remove vegetable matter from yarn so you could either dye with the dyestuff or with the liquor.

Felted wool

It is possible to dye felted wool, but be aware that as the fibres are tightly meshed the dye takes longer to penetrate.

Knitted or woven fabric

This can be dyed in a piece. Give the material plenty of space in the bath if you do this, to ensure that the fabric is dyed evenly throughout.

Silk

Silk can be treated in a similar way to wool but the temperature of the bath should be lower, otherwise the silk loses its lustre. So dyeing wool and silk at the same time could be a problem, but it is worth trying, as it will give you different shades with the same dye.

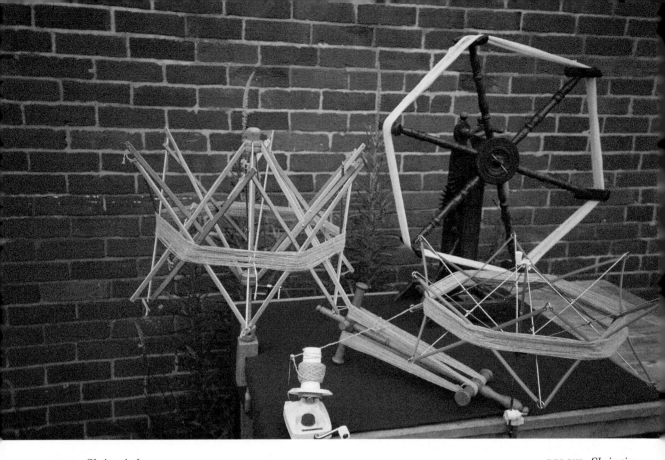

ABOVE: *Skein winders.*   BELOW: *Skein ties.*

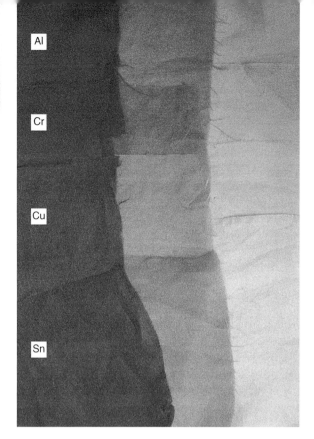

ABOVE: *Silk dyed with madder; madder and weld; weld.*

BELOW: *Silk dyed with coreopsis with mordants, Al, Cr, Cu, Sn.*

Vegetable fibres

Cotton, linen and other vegetable fibres require more preparation when mordanting: if treated like wool, the colours are less vivid and more fugitive.

PREPARING AND HANDLING WOOL AND HAIR FIBRES

Wool needs to be well scoured and free from grease. Liquid soap it ideal for this, as it leaves no trace of powder. If grease is still present, then after the mordanting process when the wool is washed, patches of the mordant have a tendency to be washed away with the remaining grease. 'Wet out' the yarn (before entering it into the mordant bath) in a weak soap solution, which does not have a lot of foam, otherwise the fibres will float to the surface. This water should be the same temperature as the mordant bath. The amount of water in the bath is not critical but it must be enough to cover the fibre and to allow movement otherwise the take-up of the

mordant will be patchy. However, when weighing the dry fibre and the mordants, try to be accurate: variation of the percentages used will affect the fastness of the colour. If too much is used, it will be wasteful as the mordant will still be present in the bath after mordanting. It is important to make sure the mordant chemicals are well dissolved in the bath before adding the wetted fibre.

Do not shock wool by sudden changes of temperature, otherwise it will felt. Bring the mordant bath up to the simmer slowly. When the mixture begins to boil, adjust the temperature to allow a gentle simmering. Do not stir vigorously when simmering. Take care not to shock the fibre by taking it out from boiling bath to cold water rinse. It is best to let the fibres cool in the bath or, if removing the fibres before this, transfer to a bath of clean water of the same temperature.

Identification of differently mordanted hanks

If using several differently mordanted yarns in the same dye bath then you may consider using a code in knotted cotton ties: one knot for alum, two for chrome, three for copper and four for tin. There may be some leakage of mordants between the samples, which may affect the colour. If the samples are well rinsed after the mordanting process there is likely to be very little cross-contamination. Similarly, if you use a copper or an aluminium dye vessel there may be some small effect on the shade. If you use an iron dye pot it is likely to sadden the colour.

HOW TO PRE-MORDANT WOOL

The percentages given refer to the amount of chemical to be used as a percentage of the weight of dry wool.

Alum

8% alum (aluminium potassium sulphate), 7% cream of tartar.

Use a small quantity of warm water to dissolve the alum and cream of tartar. Put this in a dye bath and add enough cold water to cover the fibre totally.

Place the wetted wool into the bath. Heat the bath slowly so that it comes to the boil in an hour. Simmer for a further 45 minutes. Remove from the heat and when the temperature is cool enough to handle, remove the fibre and rinse well to remove any loose alum. The wool can be used straight away or kept damp for up to five days to 'age'. Alternatively it can be dried and kept. It will be reluctant to wet when it has been dried, so make sure it is damp all through when it is eventually used. If you use too much alum the wool will feel sticky.

Chrome

1% chrome (potassium dichromate), 2% concentrated formic acid.

Chrome is poisonous and an irritant; formic acid can burn and form blisters on skin.

Fill the bath with enough cold water to cover the fibre totally and stir in the chrome and formic acid until dissolved. Place the wetted fibre into bath and put on a lid to keep in the fumes and to keep out the light. Heat the bath so that it comes to boiling in 30 minutes. Let it simmer for 45 minutes. Then remove from the heat and rinse when cool enough to handle. Use immediately. Do not dispose of the remaining mordant water down the domestic drains. The use of formic acid will mean that most of the chrome will have been absorbed into the fibre.

Copper

2% copper (copper sulphate), 2% concentrated acetic acid (so this means that if you have 100g of dry yarn, you would use 2ml of acetic acid). You could also use white wine vinegar, but bear in mind that the standard strength of white wine vinegar is weaker than the concentrated acid, so use five times the volume (therefore you would use 10ml of vinegar for 100g of dry yarn).

It will give a better fastness of colour than alum but if you use too much the light fastness is decreased. Fill the bath with enough water to cover the fibre, stir in the acid and the copper until dissolved. Place the wetted fibre in the bath and heat until boiling in 30 minutes. Simmer for 45 minutes. Remove from the heat and rinse well, once cool enough to handle. Use the fibre immediately. **NB** Copper is poisonous.

Tin

7% tin (stannous chloride), 8% oxalic acid or cream of tartar.

Tin is poisonous and makes the wool brittle. It does brighten the colour so a very small amount is often used in conjunction with the other mordants. Fill the bath with enough water to cover the fibre. If using powdered oxalic acid it will need to be dissolved in a small amount of warm water then added to the bath. If using liquid acid always add it to the water, rather than adding water to the acid. The tin will need to be dissolved in warm water before adding it to the bath. Place wetted fibre in the bath, put on a lid to reduce the fumes and heat until boiling in 30 minutes. Simmer for 45 minutes. Remove from the heat and rinse well when cool enough to handle. Use the fibre immediately.

Iron

5% ferrous sulphate.

This is usually used after the dyeing with other mordants, or a short time before the end to sadden the colour. The iron will tend to rot the fibres. The fibre will need to be removed from the bath, the iron added and dissolved and the fibre replaced. Do not leave in too long: 30 minutes should be the maximum allowed. Keep checking the colour every

5 minutes and remove when the shade required appears. Rinse thoroughly.

Post-mordanting

After the initial mordanting and dyeing process, the fibre can be added to another different mordant bath for a short time. This alters the colour: with iron it can change to a green or a brown, and if copper is used on a madder- or alum-dyed yarn, the colour is darkened to a maroon.

PREPARING AND USING THE DYE BATH

Once the fibres have been mordanted, the dyeing can begin. Make sure the container is large enough for the fibres to move freely in the liquid. Fill the dye bath with water. Either place the dye plant material directly in the water or put into a mesh bag and submerge this in the water. Wet out the fibres with a weak soap solution and put into the dye bath. Turn the heat on so that it brings the water to a simmering point slowly (with larger quantities this can take an hour). Turn the heat down so the water is just at simmering point, and keep at this temperature for an hour. Turn the heat off and leave to cool. Take the yarn out and gently squeeze out the liquid. Rinse in warm water and remove excess water with a spinner. At this point most of the plant material will shake out of the hank. Wash the yarn in

Weld plant in dye bath.

Blackberry dye bath and yarn.

warm soapy water, then rinse and spin again. Vinegar in the last rinse helps to restore the pH and sometimes brightens the colour. Then hang out to dry. The drained plant material can be put on the compost heap.

PREPARATION AND HANDLING OF SILK

Initially raw silk needs to be boiled to remove the gum. Silk, if it is still waxy, will need to be 'scoured'. This is done with 5% bicarbonate of soda dissolved in water and put into a bath with enough water to allow the silk to move freely. Place the pre-soaked silk in the bath and start heating. Do not boil, but keep the temperature to a slow simmer for an hour. Exactly how long will depend on the type of silk. If the silk is still stiff it will need longer; if limp, it has been over-scoured. It should feel 'squeaky'. As the silk is to be dyed then it is better to under-scour as the dyeing process will complete the cleaning. Rinse thoroughly at about 40°C (100°F) and hang to dry. Silk skeins tend to mat if not handled gently. If the yarn is tangled then hitting it against a flat smooth surface will help to separate the threads. When mordanting the silk the temperature should not be above 70°C (160°F).

SCOURING AND MORDANTING COTTON AND LINEN

Put the fibre into warm water to soak so that it bulks out. Add enough soap so that it wets the fibres rather than creating a lot of suds. Washing soda (caustic soda should not be used) is added in solution to the bath at a rate of 24% of the dry weight of fibre. The fibres are then put in and the temperature is brought to the boil and kept there for two hours. The bath is then removed from the heat and when cool the fibres are rinsed. It is now ready for the tannin treatment.

Tannin

The temperature in the tannin bath is kept at 60°C (140°F) for an hour then the yarn is left to cool in the bath. It is then rinsed and mordanting should take place immediately.

Alum

If alum is used at a rate of 50%, it is again kept simmering at 60°C (140°F) for an hour and left to cool in the bath.

Chrome

1% chrome and 2% formic acid is put into solution and added to the bath and the damp, tannin-treated yarn is added, brought to the boil and simmered for an hour and left to cool in the bath. The lid is kept on the pan due to the fumes and the need to restrict light (otherwise the take-up will be patchy). When taken out, the yarn will need to be rinsed to remove any surplus mordant.

Copper

2% copper and 2% acetic acid, treated in the same way as chrome.

Tin

7% tin and 8% oxalic acid, treated like chrome.

As the vegetable fibres will need to be thoroughly wetted before use, it is suggested that the dyeing process is done straight after mordanting. If the same dye is used for both animal and vegetable fibres then the colour will be paler and more fugitive on the vegetable yarn. Once dyed the fibres should be washed in soap, rinsed and dried naturally.

SAFETY PRECAUTIONS

Rubber gloves and face masks should be used.

Do not add water to concentrated acids: **always add the acid to the water.**

Keep the chemicals safely shut or locked away from children.

If dyeing with children make sure that they are aware of the dangers and are closely supervised.

Any liquids you make up must be labelled with what it is, the concentration and the date when made, particularly if you are using old drinks bottles.

Cotton dyed with safflower, and linen dyed with madder.

EXHAUST BATH

When you have completed the initial dyeing you will find that there is still dyestuff in the solution. If you put in more mordanted fibre and treat it in the same way as in the first dyeing process you will get lighter shades of the same colour. If there is too little, you will get patchy colour.

Naturally coloured wool

If you use light grey and fawn you will get a marbled effect and the colour will be of different shades within the yarn. This can be useful if you need to tone down bright shades of a colour. Yellow, orange and red on fawn gives brown tints. Blue on grey gives interesting colour variations.

SOLAR DYEING

This is done in clear glass jars with screw-top lids. A 600ml (16oz) or 1 Imperial pint (1.3 US pints) jar will hold about 25g (1oz) of fibre; larger catering jars will hold proportionally more.

There are four variations of this method:

1. Weigh the dry yarn and work out how much mordant is needed. Fill the jar with alternating layers of dye material and wetted and clean yarn. Dissolve the mordant in a little hot water in the jar; then add enough cold water to fill the jar to the brim. Put cling film over the mouth of the jar and screw the top on. Place on a drip tray on a sunny window sill. Depending on the strength of the sun, the yarn should start to show colour

ABOVE: *White, fawn and grey yarn and fleece with samples of dye.*

BELOW: *White, fawn and grey wool dyed with alum and coreopsis.*

White

Fawn

Grey

Solar dyeing with weld with alum.

Solar dyed fibres dyed with weld/alum: silk, felt, wool yarn.

Solar dyeing with madder and alum.

Solar-dyed fibres with madder/alum: silk, felt, wool yarn.

after about a week. Once dyed the yarn is removed, rinsed and dried.

2. Pre-mordanted yarn could be used. Make sure this is well wetted before continuing with the interleaving process described above.

3. The dissolved mordant and the dye material are put in the jar for a week in the sun, then the liquor is drained off. The un-mordanted yarn or fibre is added to the jar with the liquor and left for a further week. Once dyed the yarn is rinsed and dried.

4. If a liquor is made of the dye material in a dye pan, a greater concentration of colour will be present and there will be more space for the yarn. This method would be particularly useful for wool rovings because removing bits of dye material is tedious. Pre-mordanted yarn could be used or the mordant could be put in the jar as described in method 1.

Sometimes the mixture will ferment; this smells dreadful but will still dye. Sometimes a duller colour will be produced, and at other times the decomposition may change the chemical process and then, for example, an orange may be obtained rather than an expected yellow. Mould growth does not seem to affect the colour, but will take a little longer to rinse clean. It has been found that if madder is used with the fibre, where the root is in contact with the material there will be a spot that is a darker shade of red.

Light fastness

Mordanting will make the colour light fast. To test how fast the colour is, put a sample wrapped on a card and half cover in a sunny window for a month. If you are making a garment then the chances are that it will be in a drawer or a dark cupboard when not being worn, so any fading will be minimal. A wall hanging or a rug will be more likely to be exposed to the sunshine so in this case, testing is important.

Light fastness test of wrapping of dyed fibre in window.

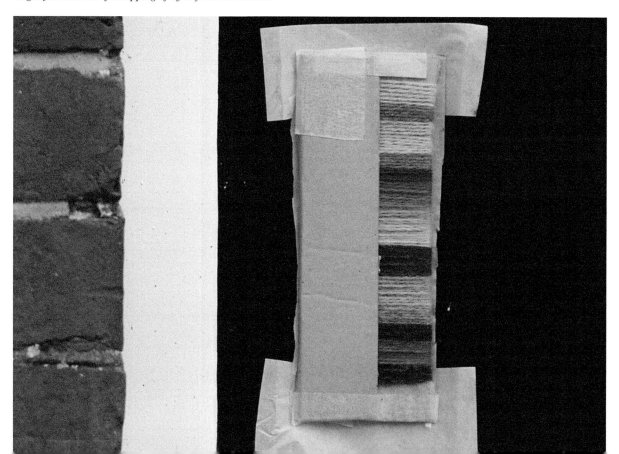

Wrapping showing faded colours after two summer months.

CHAPTER 3

Natural dyeing felt

Felt is a fabric made from randomly distributed un-spun fibres. It is a technique for making textiles which pre-dates spun yarn. The frozen graves in the Pazyryk valley in the Altai Mountains date from 2,500 years ago, and it was here that felt was found preserved in the permafrost. The collection is now at the Hermitage Museum in St Petersburg. The dyed felts recovered show a colourful depiction of life at that time with animals and people. The designs are appliquéd on to a surface so they are sharply defined.

FELT MADE FROM FIBRES

Felt made from fine wool fibres is easier to make than felt made from coarse fibres. Smooth fibres such as hair and silk need to be trapped by wool fibres if they are to be incorporated in a surface design. Sheep and goat fibres can be a variety of colours from grey to black and from fawn to dark brown. These colours tend to fade in sunlight so for more permanent colours it is better to dye white fibres. Kemp, which is hollow, brittle and like a short white hair will not felt or take colour. If incorporated into a garment it will tend to make the surface scratchy.

Commercial chemically dyed fibres tend to be uniform and consistent in colour. As the fibres have been scoured in hot water with harsh chemicals to remove dirt and grease and then machine carded, they tend to have lost some of the elasticity and crimp which is present when handwashed and carded. Felt made by hand tends to be softer with more loft. This is when the felt retains more spring because the crimps in the fibre have not been straightened out by industrial scouring and the mechanical felting process, which uses heavy rollers or plates. The effect is that the felt feels thicker, which means that the felting process takes more time.

Natural plant dyes are consistent within the same bath but will vary from batch to batch, which makes matching or reproducing colours difficult. Animal fibres will take dye but mordants are needed to make them permanent. The fibres need to be free of grease and dirt, otherwise the dye take-up will be inconsistent. The main problem is to prevent the fibres from felting during the mordanting and the dyeing process. Dye plant materials are more difficult to remove from loose fibres than from yarn. So either the fibres can be put into a mesh bag that allows them to move freely, or only dye liquor is used. (This is made by boiling up the plant then sieving out the residue and using only the coloured solution.)

You must treat the fibre gently:

- do not change temperatures in the dye bath rapidly;
- do not agitate the fibres or squeeze them vigorously;
- do not run cold water directly on to the fibres; and
- do not use a tumble dryer to dry the fibre.

A spinner or a cycle in the washing machine that spins but does not add water can be useful. This cuts down the amount of water and makes the fibre easier to handle.

There are several different options regarding at what point you dye the fibre:

- as raw uncarded but washed fleece;

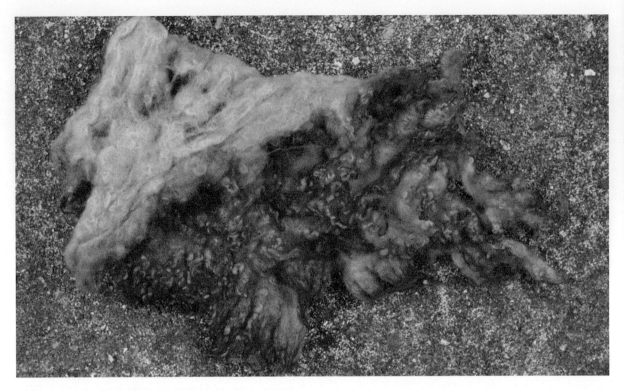

Partially madder-dyed fleece.

- as raw carded fibre either as tops (long slivers of about 10cm in diameter) or in batts (sheets that are as wide as the carding machine rollers);
- as half felts;
- as fully felted pieces.

STEP-BY-STEP GUIDE TO DYEING FIBRES FOR FELT

1a. Clean the fibres by washing in warm or hand hot soapy water. Lay the fleece in the water, leave to soak for 15 minutes, then gently lift out and spin. Return to clean water to rinse, and keep this process going until the water is clear. Remove any contaminants such as vegetation or heavily soiled fibres. Urine-soaked fibres will take the mordants and the dyes in a different way so will be a different colour from the rest of the fleece.

1b. If fibres are already clean and dry, weigh them. Then they will need to be wetted out before mordanting. Run a bowl of hand hot water and put a few drops of liquid soap in, then gently put the fibres or felt in and leave to soak for up to two hours. This opens out the fibres and means that the mordant will be more evenly taken up.

2. Mordant by one of the methods described in Chapter 2, but raise the temperature gradually to simmering (this can take up to an hour or more), then keep it at this temperature, just below boiling, for another hour. Once completed, take off the heat, leave to cool overnight, then spin and rinse to remove any loose mordant. If you have used the 8% alum and 7% cream of tartar then there should be very little alum left in the water of the mordant bath and so this can be tipped down the drain or into a soakaway. It is possible to use a cooler bath, so dissolve the mordant and the assist in hot water, add this to enough warm water to cover the fibres and leave for twelve days, turning every three days, then

Half-felts used to give clear lines of colour.

spin and rinse in warm water, drying by rolling in a towel to remove excess liquid.

3. The dye materials need to be brought to the boil and the colour extracted. Sieve out dye plant material and leave to cool, then put in the wetted fibre and bring to the boil, again simmering gently until dyed. If using the mesh bag you can either put the fibres or the dye material in with the initial extraction process, but make sure the fibres have room to move, otherwise the dye will not penetrate the centre. It is possible to use a gentler method: this involves pouring the cool dye liquor over the fibres and pressing it in to help penetrate and leaving in a polythene bag for several weeks. Otherwise you could try steaming or using a microwave. These methods do not produce such vivid colours as the simmering.

4. When the dye process is complete, leave fibres in the bath to cool, then rinse in warm soapy water and continue rinsing until the water is clear. Be careful not to felt at this stage by rough treatment and rapid change of temperature.

5. To dry the fibres, spread them on a rack. Be careful they don't blow away: pegging individual locks may help.

6. Once dry, the fibre can be carded and blended to obtain the colour desired.

Half felts

This is where the fibres are partially felted, so it holds together but is not felted; the designs are then cut out. This method is used where a clear line between colours is required. If roughly handled they might turn into fully felted pieces.

Needle felt

This is a process that is carried out on dry fibres with special hooked needles. What happens is that the hooks drag individual fibres through the felt to form a firm fabric. This means that non-animal fibres and hair can be incorporated into the work. If dyeing needle felt that has been made from a mixture of fibres, be aware that these may either not take the dye or produce another shade or tone of the same colour. Equally, if a mixture of fibres have been mordanted with many of the chemicals mentioned above, then they will produce different shades. Needle felts can be very solid, which will mean that the wetting out process, the mordanting and the dyeing will take longer to soak in to the depths.

Fully felted fabrics

These tend to be dense; the dyeing will therefore take longer and will sometimes not penetrate into

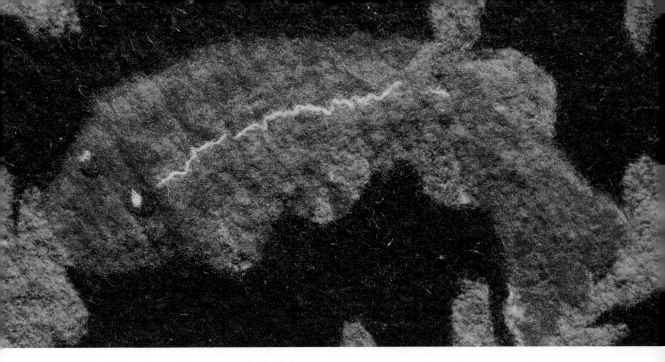

Needle-felted fibres to keep colours separate in the design.

the middle. Dyeing at this stage can mean that the whole fabric will be the same colour. This can be useful if you want a consistent backing for appliquéd felt. It is possible to partially dip the fabric, which means that you can get a gradation of colour. Care must be taken at this stage, as colour will migrate upwards out of the bath, so a clear definition of colour is not possible. Indigo and woad would lend themselves to this technique but care must be taken not to introduce air into the vat. Interesting effects can be achieved if different mordants are used before felting and dyeing. Resists such as elastic bands and plastic ties can be used to create other designs. Once dyed, the fibres could be laid together so that the edges will show those colours. If thick enough these layers can be cut into revealing glimpses of the underlying shades. Different fibres will give a variety of effects: Wensleydale will have a sheen and a brighter colour, and Shetland and Merino will take the dye in different ways and produce different shades of the same colour when in the same dye bath. The feel of the felt will differ, depending on the fibres used. Silk tends to take colour better than wool, so even if it is in the same felt with the same mordants in the same dye bath, it will look different.

Knitted dyed yarn, comparing unfelted and felted samples.

Felting with already dyed yarn

When a piece of knitting with dyed yarn is to be felted, a sample test will help to work out the shrinkage after the felting process. Provided your yarn has not shrunk during the dyeing, the amount of shrinkage will depend on the type of fleece and the thickness of the yarn. The colours should not be affected by the felting if the yarn has been well mordanted and rinsed before knitting. Indigo and woad are surface dyes and have a tendency to rub off on fingers when the yarn is knitted.

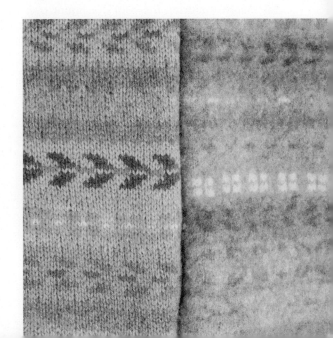

CHAPTER 4

Dye plant illustrations and information

The following fifty-four plants used for various dyeing processes are those that can be grown in gardens or collected easily. They are in alphabetical order by their most common names. Where there are other names they have been included. The Latin name is given: some plants have two names attached as both varieties can be used but the first one listed is the one illustrated by the botanical watercolour.

There is a description for each plant with historical information, planting and growing instructions, and finally specific instructions for the dyeing with that plant. The mordanting and actual dye procedures have already been described.

The wrapped cardboard bobbins are of 100% wool and in the sequence from top to bottom of alum (Al), chrome (Cr), copper (Cu) and tin (Sn). If there is an un-mordanted sample it will appear above the alum sample.

Several dye plants have been used which do not produce good colours on wool; in this case cotton and silk have been dyed.

The colours are those I achieved from the plants grown in my garden in Hampshire and dyed using water from there. Given different climatic and soil conditions, plus variations in quantity of dye materials, length of heating and type of wool, the colours shown can only be a guide.

I have used tin and chrome as mordants so that it can be seen that similar colours can be dyed using alum or copper or oxalic acid and other plants.

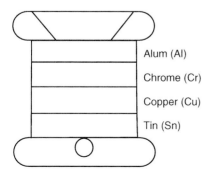

Alum (Al)

Chrome (Cr)

Copper (Cu)

Tin (Sn)

Sample yarn bobbin showing order of mordants and orientation.

AGRIMONY

(Church steeples, Sticklewort) *Agrimonia eupatoria, Agrimonia odorata*

Agrimony was used by the Anglo-Saxons as a wound healer and by the Greeks as a general tonic but also for curing dysentery and snake bites. The juice has been used on animals as an insect repellent. The leaves prevent bread from going mouldy. The name 'Sticklewort' refers to the burrs on the seeds, which attach themselves to clothing and fur. The sweet scent of the dried whole plant has been used to make herbal pillows.

This perennial grows on dry chalky soils as a low plant but up to 60cm on loam in damper conditions in the sun or semi-shade. The plant tolerates very alkaline soils and does best in sunny positions. It can be grown from seed in the autumn in a greenhouse or cold frame and planted out in the spring, or planted *in situ*. Clumps can be divided in the spring or autumn or root cuttings can be taken in winter. It flowers from June to August and the seeds ripen from August to October. The seeds have hooks on, which means that they are naturally spread on animal fur or clothes. Agrimony is pollinated by bees, flies, moths and butterflies, particularly the Peacock butterfly. It has a pleasant smell when dried, like spicy apricot.

The leaves and stalks are gathered in September and give shades from beige to orange-brown. If gathered later the colour is darker. The dried flower heads produce butter yellow with alum and tin and a yellow-green with copper. The root produces a pale yellow colour.

Agrimony plant.

Sample of dyes – entire agrimony plant and flowers.

ALKANET

(Dyer's bugloss) *Anchusa* or *Alkanna tinctoria*

Alkanet was used by Egyptians and Greeks as a cosmetic and to stain leather. The red colour has been used in thermometers and for litmus to test for acid and alkali. The dye is used as a stain for wood to make it look like rosewood or mahogany.

Alkanet is an evergreen perennial that grows up to 30cm (1ft) tall and has small bright blue-purple flowers in the summer. Plants can be grown from seed in midsummer, or the roots can be divided in spring or autumn, or by root cuttings taken in late winter. It grows well in rich soil and needs to be well watered and will grow in both full sun and semi-shade. It does well in alkaline soil and will tolerate drought and salt air. If the soil is too wet over winter the roots will rot. The plant can be cut back after flowering.

Root bark collected in the autumn is used for red dye with alcohol diluted with water. When using alum as a mordant, keep the temperature below 60°C (140°F) for one hour; this gives lavender and purple, and when rinsed in vinegar, a red colour is produced. Deep shades of grey, violet and purple can be achieved by boiling a small amount of methylated spirits or rubbing alcohol, then diluting this with enough water to cover the wool or silk, and finally using 50g of root to 100g of wool. Unfortunately, the colours have poor light and wash fastness.

Alkanet plant.

Sample of dyes – alkanet (no mordant, Al mordant, methylated spirits, rinsed in water) and alkanet (no mordant, Al mordant, acetic acid and rinsed in water).

BARBERRY
Berberis vulgaris

Barberry was used in Darjeeling by Tibetan refugees for dyeing, and in the dye for tents in Turkey during the First World War. In Poland the bark of the root is used to colour leather. The unripe berries have been used as beads.

This deciduous bushy shrub grows up to 3m (10ft) tall and is often used as a hedging plant, particularly as it has thorns. It grows in most conditions but prefers a sunny position on chalk soil. It will tolerate coastal conditions. It is not frost tender and is in leaf from March to November, flowers in May and June and sets its red berries in September and October. It grows from berries and from cuttings and suckers.

When the roots and bark are chopped up and used, a good yellow-orange is obtained with alum. It has good light fastness. When used with chrome the colour is a good rich brown. In the summer, the tops of the new shoots when boiled will give a range of golds.

Barberry in winter.

Sample of dyes – barberry whole plant and green shoots.

BIRCH

Betula pendula

The wood is strong and hard but not sufficiently durable for outside use. The twigs are used for brooms, and the bark has tannins that are used to tan leather. The sap is fermented to make alcohol. The bark from the *Betula papyrifera* is used to make birch bark canoes.

Birch trees grow on poorer sandy or limey soils reaching a height of 25m (80ft) on a single trunk. They are relatively quick growing but short lived at around forty years. The young saplings can be bought at most garden centres.

The chopped twigs will give yellow-green with alum. The leaves in late June give the yarn a straw gold colour and when simmered longer give deeper colours. The bark when cut up and soaked for several days gives pinky browns and black when rinsed with iron.

The painting opposite illustrates *Betula utilis*.

Birch bark.

Sample of dyes – birch bark and leaves.

BISTORT

(Patience dock, Kitchen witch,
Adderwort, Dragonswort, Red legs,
Sweet dock) *Polygonum bistorta*

The name *bistorta* comes from the double twisted root. The high tannin content in the root means that it has been used as a substitute for oak bark for tanning leather. In Russia, when the tannin is removed from the root, it is ground and used as a flour substitute in bread. The dried powdered leaves were used to kill worms in children. If animals eat it in excess it can cause photo-sensitivity.

The bistort can be grown by root division in spring or autumn. The seeds are sown in spring or autumn. The sap can cause skin irritation so care must be taken.

The fact that the roots contain oxalic acid means that colours can be produced without mordants but with them it will give a greater variety of colours. The flowers will give a yellow colour, the leaves a khaki colour, and the roots a pinky brown and black when rinsed with iron.

Bistort plant and flowers.

Sample of dyes – bistort root, leaves and leaves and iron.

BLACKBERRY

(Bramble) *Rubus fruticosus*

The Romans used the leaves to make a tea, as they are a good remedy for dysentery.

It is a common hedgerow plant and the blackberry has provided a useful source of food for centuries.

There are many different varieties of bramble. It grows in rich moist soils and full sun. It can be grown from seed, by root division or by suckers. The long trailing shoots will root where they touch the ground. The plants are long lived and can be cut back. As the blackberry flowers late it tends not to be affected by frost so can be grown in areas prone to late frosts. The new canes are best planted in autumn when the ground is still warm so that they become established before spring.

The roots can be chopped up and boiled and will give orange. The young spring shoots produce light yellowy greens. The more mature leaves when cut up and boiled give a good dark green when treated with iron after the initial yellow. It is best to use the berries as soon as they are ripe. If they are mashed up and then gently brought to simmer, dark pink can be obtained from alum and, with iron, a blue-grey. They have poor light fastness and the alum-iron combination fades to a fawn, although with tin then iron it stays lilac. The colour is sensitive to acid and alkali and will change when rinsed in one of these.

Blackberry fruit and yarn sample.

Sample of dyes – blackberry new shoots, leaves, leaves with iron and berries (no mordant, Al, Cr, Sn).

BLACKTHORN

(Sloe) *Prunus spinosa*

Sloe berries have been found in Iron Age burials, implying they were a food source. They are used to make sloe gin. The wood, which is hard and tough, is used for marquetry, wood turning and walking sticks.

Blackthorn is large shrub growing up to 4m (13ft) tall with long thorns, which, if they puncture the skin, can cause the wound to become septic. For this reason it is often planted as a vandal-proof hedge. The white blossom appears in early spring. The sloes are gathered in the autumn. The leaves contain small amounts of hydrogen cyanide, which is poisonous and has a bitter taste. It is an invasive shrub and spreads by suckering. It can be grown from berries.

Bark is chopped and soaked for a week. When used with alum it gives orange-brown or black colours. The blossom, which can be used either fresh or dried, gives a golden yellow and orange depending which mordant is used. The sap wood produces yellow colours and the heartwood brown. The leaves with alum give a green. Sloe berries will produce a pale lilac with alkali rinse and pink with an acid rinse, but they are not very light fast.

Blackthorn blossom.

Sample of dyes – blackthorn leaves and blossom.

BROOM

(Lady's slipper, Cat's paw) *Cytisus scoparius* or *Sarothamus scoparius*

The Crusaders wore a spray of broom in their helmets. The Plantagenets took their name from its Latin name, *planta genista*. Shepherds in the Auvergne thought that it protected their sheep from snake bites, in fact it contains an alkaloid which does just that. The stem contains tannins so has been used to tan leather. The twigs are made into brooms, hence its connection with witches. The bark fibre is made into paper. The flower buds, when pickled, are a substitute for capers.

This is a hardy perennial shrub, which grows well in dry sandy soil in a sunny position up to 3m (10ft) tall. It will tolerate very acid soils, salt air, atmospheric pollution and very low temperatures. It can be grown from seed in the spring; these need to be soaked for a day in warm water then cold stratified (put in a plastic bag with moistened paper towel and refrigerated) for a month. They are then planted in the greenhouse until summer when they are put into their permanent positions. Mature plants do not transplant well. Half-ripe wood cuttings can be taken in spring or mature wood cuttings in late summer. The profusion of flowers appears from May to June and the seeds ripen from August to November. It can be pruned in July after flowering and is often used as a hedging plant. It is attractive to butterflies such as the Green Hairstreak. It attracts insects away from nearby plants.

The fresh flowers with alum give yellow. If an iron after-bath is used for five minutes it turns green. The fresh shoots with chrome give a warm green and with copper a dark green. The bark when chopped and boiled produces a yellowy brown.

Broom bush.

Sample of dyes – broom shoots and flowers.

COREOPSIS

(Tickseed, Calliopsis) *Coreopsis tinctoria*

One old book recommends sowing this plant 'within three days of the new moon'. Originally it came from North America where it is known as tickseed.

There are both biennial and perennial varieties. This half-hardy plant grows in temperate climates to a height of 50cm (1ft 7in) in ordinary soil in a sunny or semi-shaded, well-drained position. Sow in late spring in its final position as it does not transplant well. It can be grown under glass, as it needs a long growing season, so plant in March in the greenhouse. It will need to be protected against frost and slugs. Plant 20cm (8in) apart and keep well watered in dry weather. It flowers between June and September: use fresh flowers, removing as they flower as this encourages more to grow. It is a plant that attracts bees. The seeds ripen from June to October.

The flowers are used and with alum produce a good rich orange; with chrome, a foxy red; with copper, a good dark tan; and with tin, golds. All of these have a good light fastness. This dye is sensitive to pH, an acid rinse will give reds and an alkali rinse with either washing soda or ammonia keeps the yellow hues. If using dried flowers, only half the weight is needed compared with fresh flowers. This is one way to be able to continue dyeing out of season when fresh plants are not available.

Coreopsis flowers.

Coreopsis used to dye yarn for Tam o' Shanter.

Sample of dyes – coreopsis flowers.

DAFFODIL

(Lent lily) *Narcissus pseudonarcissus*

This is a native plant of Europe. Narcissus was a youth in Greek legend who fell in love with his own reflection in water, pined away and where he died the narcissus grew. Daffodils were used to dye linen and hessian in Medieval times.

The daffodil grows from a bulb in most conditions, provided it does not dry out. They can be grown from seed, in which case there will be flowers in the second year. The bulbs are best when planted or split after the leaves have died back. They flower in the spring. The flower and the bulb contain toxins that affect the nervous system and can paralyse the heart, so do not confuse them with onions. The sap is an irritant and can cause dermatitis. The flower has a pleasant perfume.

The flowers are best collected in dry weather when they are fully open. They are then put into a bath with enough water to cover and brought to the boil. The wool is dyed a good yellow with alum and chrome, and a bright yellow with tin. If the wool is then dipped in an after-bath of iron, it will turn green.

Daffodil dye bath.

Sample of dyes – daffodil flower.

DAHLIA

Dahlia variabilis

These are thought to have originated from Mexico in damp woodlands. The tubers have been eaten as a vegetable and contain a sweetener which is suitable for diabetics.

This is a half-hardy tuberous perennial. It grows to a height of 1.5m (5ft) with many different types of flowers. The dahlia grows in good well-manured soils in well-drained sunny positions but needs to be kept moist so it should be watered regularly during dry spells. Tubers are planted 8cm (3in) apart in late spring and early summer. If the winters are severe, tubers need to be lifted and stored in a frost-free place. It can be grown from seed sown in late winter or early spring: germination can take up to fourteen days. Seedlings need to be kept moist and warm and planted out into peat pots, which reduces root disturbance. They will need to be overwintered inside, to be planted out in their second year after the risk of late frosts has passed. Tubers can be divided as long as each section has a growing point.

One can dye with flowers in bloom or with dried heads. The strength of the colour will depend on the proportion of dye to fibre. For a strong colour use the same weight of flowers to wool. With alum the fibres are a creamy yellow with a fair light fastness but with chrome, which gives a good brassy orange, it has a good light fastness. With tin, a yellow-orange is obtained.

Shades of yellow.

Sample of dyes – dahlia flowers.

DAMSON

Prunus domestica

The name came from its origins in Damascus. The 'Ice Man' (dated to the Neolithic period of 5,300 years ago), whose body was found in the Austrian Oetzal Alps in 1991, carried them. Damson stones have been found in Roman sites and in the Viking settlement of Yorvik in York. Slivovitz is an alcoholic drink made from fermented plum juice and is the national drink of Serbia. The skins were used to dye cotton purple. There are records of damsons being sent from the village of Bishop's Wood in Shropshire to Liverpool, to be used as dye for naval uniforms.

Damsons are thought to be a hybrid between sloe and cherry plum. The modern cultivars such as Merryweather and Cherry damson can be used for dyeing. The tree grows up to 15m (50ft) tall; if it is a domestic variety it will depend on which root stock has been used. It grows in most soils and is tolerant of altitude, salt air and climate. The tree grows best in limestone soils. It is used as a shelter-belt hedge and as a pollinator in commercial orchards. It is susceptible to honey fungus. It lives up to fifty years and can be grown from suckers. A tree will start cropping at eight years old. It is in blossom in April and the plums ripen in October. The fruit is best after the first frosts. It is pollinated by bees and insects. Pollination is best in damp conditions. It can be grown from the stones but they need protecting from mice.

The damson fruit will produce plum red with tin as a mordant, but with alum, yellow which fades to fawn. The addition of vinegar or oxalic acid reveals the pinks and purples. The bark, when sliced off the wood and soaked for several days will dye wool orange with alum and chrome; and with copper, brown.

Sample of dyes – damson bark and fruit.

DANDELION
(Peasant's clock) *Taraxacum officinalis*

The name may have derived from the French '*dent-de-leon*', referring to the deeply toothed leaves. It has long been used as a diuretic. The roots have been roasted as a substitute for coffee. The milky latex has been used as a mosquito repellent but can cause dermatitis. As the plant is high in potassium, the flowers are a good bacterial activator for the compost bin. The juice is supposed to fade freckles. The leaves are eaten as a green salad and if blanched lose their bitterness. It is useful as a winter salad; the young leaves have a high content of vitamins A and C and contain iron and calcium.

This common weed grows everywhere including in marine conditions. It grows to 45cm (1ft 6in) tall and flowers throughout the year with the seeds ripening after successive flowerings. It is pollinated by insects. Its long tap root makes it difficult to eradicate. It is attractive to bees, moths and butterflies. It can be grown from seed but will need a deep pot for its tap root. If the top of the plant is removed it re-grows with multiple heads.

The flowers are gathered in full sun to give yellowy green. The roots, when dug up and washed then chopped into small pieces and boiled, give a light brown. In Scotland, the roots have been used to colour tartans magenta: it may be the type of soil and variety of dandelion which give this colour.

Sample of dyes – dandelion root and flowers.

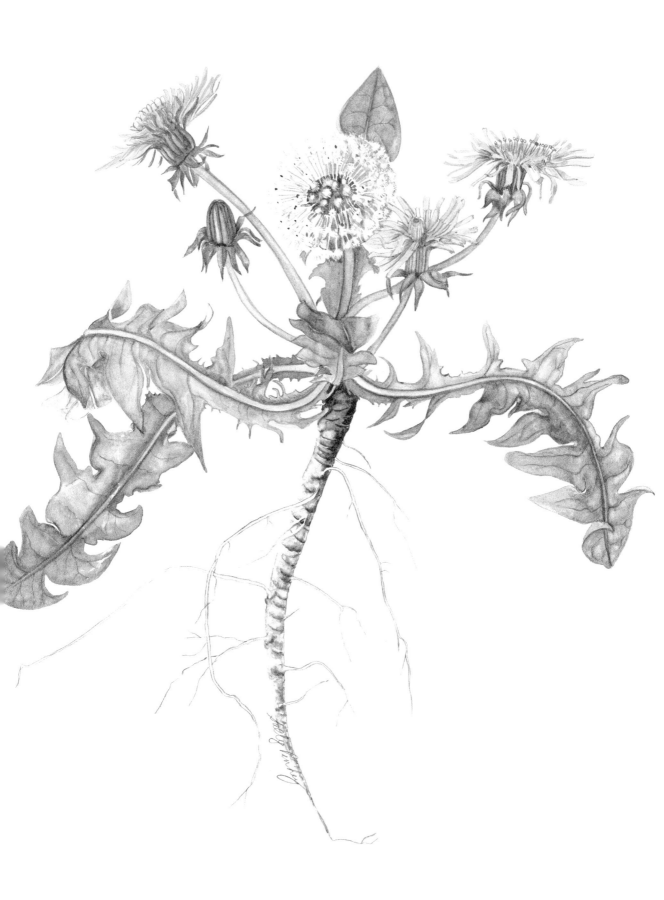

DOCK

Rumex obtusifolius

In Tibet, Peru and Bolivia the leaves are used as mordants as they are rich in tannins. The roasted seeds have been used as a coffee substitute.

The dock can be grown from rhizomes or seed, collected in the spring or the autumn. The long tap roots make it hard to get rid of as when the tops are removed multiple plants re-grow. The flowers are hermaphrodite and are wind pollinated. The dock is attractive to many insects, the Large Copper butterfly lays its eggs on the leaves and the caterpillars feed on them, then they pupate hidden under the dead leaves on the stem.

The plant contains oxalic acid so does not need a mordant but for more shades of colour other mordants can be used. If fresh or powdered roots are used with alum then the colours obtained are light brown-orange and with chrome, pinky browns. In higher concentration a good range of browns are achieved. The leaves with alum give gold, and with iron mossy green. With chrome there is a red-brown which when iron is used in the rinse gives a chestnut brown. These have a good light and wash fastness. In Ireland and Scotland the dock root is used with iron to produce black.

Dock plant and sample.

Sample of dyes – dock root (Al, Cr, Cu), soaked root, leaves and leaves with iron.

DYER'S CHAMOMILE

Anthemis tinctoria

The flowers were used as a shampoo for blonde hair to add highlights. An infusion of the flowers was used on skin to soothe insect bites and stings.

It is a herbaceous perennial which grows well from seed up to 60cm (2ft) tall. It has a pungent scent that is said to keep mosquitoes at bay. It can be grown as an annual on well-drained soils in a sunny position. It is lime intolerant and when grown in shady conditions the dyes seem to be less strong. It is more luxuriant in its second year.

When the whole plant is used it dyes a range of yellows. If large quantities of the plant are used then a denser colour is obtained. Pick the flower heads when in bloom as this encourages more flowers to grow. They need to be well dried before storing. The dried flower heads give golden yellow with alum, tan with chrome, rich brown with copper and orange with tin.

Flowers.

Sample of dyes – Dyer's chamomile leaves and flowers.

DYER'S GREENWEED

(Dyer's Broom, Woadwaxen) *Genista tinctoria*

Traces of dyer's greenweed have been found on archaeological sites. Traces have also been found in Medieval textiles. If cows eat it, it taints the milk. Historically it was one of the main sources of yellow to be used with blue to create green, hence the name 'woadwaxen'. As the textile ages the yellow tends to fade and this results in what appears to be blue grass and trees on some tapestries.

This hardy perennial bush is widespread in temperate climates. It grows to a height of 30cm to 60cm (1ft to 2ft). It does well in a good well-drained soil in full sun. It does not transplant well. Its roots have nodules which are nitrogen fixing so it improves the conditions for nearby plants. It can be grown from seed, which will need soaking for twenty-four hours in water or filing lightly before sowing. Half ripe cuttings can be taken in July and August and ripe wood cuttings in September and October.

The flowers contain the most dye but the stems can be used. Harvesting is in June and July when the plants are flowering. They can be used either fresh or dried. The colour is of excellent light and wash fastness. With alum it gives a good yellow, chrome a deeper yellow-orange, with copper a greenish yellow, and with tin a butter yellow. If pre-mordanted, then dyed blue with woad or indigo and rinsed to remove any loose blue, then dyed with greenweed, it gives Kendal green.

Dyer's greenweed in full flower.

Sample of dyes – Dyer's greenweed tops and flowers, top dyed with madder and top dyed with indigo.

ELDER

Sambucus nigra

The wood is hard and strong and is used to make combs and toys. The stems, after the pith was removed, were used to make flutes and pipes and the sambuca, the triangular stringed instrument that gave its name to the plant. The pith is used to absorb oil and dirt and is used by watchmakers. The dye has been used as ink, the flowers made into champagne and the berries into wine; in Kent it was made into 'British wine'. In Victorian times it was sold hot in winter on the streets of London. The leaves are an insect repellent when rubbed onto the skin. Sprays of flowers were tucked into horse bridles to deter flies. The flowers are a compost activator.

This shrub is found in hedgerows and waste ground. Individual trees reach up to 10m (40ft) tall. It is tolerant of salt air and is used as a shelterbelt plant. It is resistant to honey fungus. It grows well on chalk and fruits are best from plants in a sunny position. If cut down to the base it will grow again. It is resistant to rabbits but attractive to insects. Its seeds are spread by birds and animals, which eat the berries. To grow from seed it is best to plan for a two-month cold stratification then plant on into pots and out in the late spring. Half-ripe cuttings can be taken in July and August and mature cuttings in the autumn. Suckers can be replanted in the winter. The blossom appears in May and the berries in late August and September.

The bruised berries give pale lilac or blue depending on the time simmered and the amount used. If the bath is alkaline then greens are obtained, and if made acid with vinegar the red

Elderflower blossom.

colours are enhanced. With alum, blues are obtained, and with chrome, purple. Shredded leaves when boiled will give khaki and grey-green shades. The elder blossoms give vibrant yellows with alum and tin, gold with chrome, and a dark yellow-brown with copper. If the yarn is then rinsed in iron the yellows darken to golden brown.

Elderberries.

Sample of dyes – elder leaves, flowers, flowers and iron and berries.

FERN

(Mala Fern) *Dryopteris filix-mas*

Ferns are found as fossils from the Devonian period onwards. Today they are sometimes used to absorb heavy metals and arsenic from the soil.

There is a wide variety of species of fern, and they do not all grow in moist and shady woodlands. The stems grow from underground rhizomes. Ferns are widely used as ground cover and they have a range of attractive leaf shapes and colours. They grow best in acid to neutral soils.

The leaves are chopped up and boiled; initially the leaves produce a range of dark fawns. If an iron rinse is used on the fawns then warm greens are obtained. If the yarn is left in the dye bath with the leaves for twelve hours then rich browns are achieved. This is because the leaves contain iron, which deepens the colours.

A fern growing in the shade by a stream.

Sample of dyes – mala fern fresh fiddleheads and tops soaked for twelve hours.

GOLDENROD

(Aaron's rod, Woundwort) *Soldago canadensis*

The native British *solidago* is of a medium size, and has small deep yellow daisy-like flowers, which are more sparse than those of the goldenrod that we now know. The most common plant grown these days came from North America. The *soldago canadensis* is made into an infusion to make the aromatic Blue Mountain tea. The woody stems do not burn well, so were formerly used for the making of bellows. The plant has antiseptic properties and was used externally to heal wounds. The word *solidago* means 'to make whole'. Goldenrod is particularly good for mouth ulcers and sore throats. The roots were used as a poultice for burns.

Goldenrod is a tall perennial herb, growing up to 2m (6ft 6in). It spreads by horizontal stolons (stems that take root in the ground). It is very invasive, so should be grown in isolation or somewhere where its spread can be restricted. It should be lifted and split every three years or so, otherwise it becomes too restricted. It flowers from August to October and the seeds ripen in September and October. Goldenrod is pollinated by insects and is self-fertile. As the pollen is heavy and therefore not dispersed by wind, goldenrod is a plant that hay fever and asthma sufferers could grow in their gardens without ill-effect. It is attractive to butterflies, lacewings, hoverflies and ladybirds. It dies back in the autumn and reappears in spring as tiny red shoots. It can be grown by root division or by seed, sown in early spring or in November and overwintered under glass. It will grow in a wide variety of soils.

For dyeing, the most vivid yellows are achieved by using the flower heads as they are opening. These are chopped and used in the dye pot. If you use equal quantities of plant material and wool, you will obtain the strongest shades of yellow. If just the stalks are used, then more muted yellows are produced, which can be turned into mossy greens with an after-bath of iron. Chrome-mordanted wool produces a deep gold.

Sample of dyes – goldenrod top of plant.

GORSE
(Furze, Whin) *Ulex europaeus*

Gorse flowering in December.

This was used for sweeping chimneys and for fuel for brickworks and bakeries. In Scotland it was used to feed sheep and cattle. Its roots help to stabilize soils, and it is fast growing. The soaked seeds are said to be good against fleas.

Common gorse flowers between January and June; Western gorse from July to November. It makes an impenetrable barrier when grown as a hedge or as a windbreak. If not grazed it will spread and has to be controlled by burning. If grown from seed in pots in spring it can be moved to its final position later in the year (it does not transplant well). It can be pruned hard back in the autumn, and is resistant to honey fungus. It is attractive to butterflies and caterpillars such as the Green Hairstreak.

It is advisable to use thick gloves and secateurs to gather the flowers. Twigs, leaves and blossom give gold with alum. Tin produces a vivid orange. The flowers can be dried for later use. If using the shoots the thorns tend to tangle in the yarn or fibre: a tough cotton bag could be used, or you could boil the plant in water and produce a solution that can then be used for the dyeing.

Sample of dyes – gorse flowers.

GREAT MULLEIN

(Aaron's rod, Hag taper, Pig's taper)
Verbascum thapsus

This plant has had many uses, from a medicine that kills tapeworm to a hair dye used by Roman women to enhance light hair. The long flower stalks were dried, stripped of outer skin except for a narrow piece left to give the spike rigidity then dipped in tallow and used as torches, often at funerals. The leaves have been used in poultices to draw splinters. The dried down on the leaves is used as tinder. Pliny noted that figs wrapped in the leaves did not rot.

It is a hardy biennial and grows up in a spire-like stalk up to 2.4m (8ft) tall in well-drained sandy or chalk soils in sun or shade. It flowers from June to August and the seeds ripen in August and September. Flies, moths and butterflies pollinate the flowers. It will grow well from self-sown seeds. These seedlings will transplant when three or four leaves have grown. Seeds can also be sown after the danger of frost in late spring. Harvest in the summer until the first frosts. It grows as a rosette in the

Great mullein rosette.

first year then has a sturdy stalk in the second. It is attractive to both bees and butterflies, but in particular to the Mullein moth caterpillars: these can strip the leaves to their ribs.

The leaves and stalks are cut up and simmered with the fibres and produce yellow with alum, gold with chrome and a bright yellow with tin. When acid is added to the rinse the yellow turns green; if an alkali is added it turns brown. This plant dye is good for wool, cotton and linen.

Mullein in bloom.

Sample of dyes – great mullein tops.

GYPSYWORT

(Egyptian herb, Bugleweed) *Lycopus europaeus*

The gypsywort was supposed to have been used by gypsies to tan skin. The leaves have been used as poultices to cleanse infected wounds.

This is a perennial and grows to 35cm (1ft 2in) tall and spreads by rhizomes in damp soils on water margins in the sun. It flowers from June to September and the seeds ripen from August to October. It is pollinated by bees and flies but is self-fertile. It can be divided in spring or autumn or can be grown from seed.

The roots collected in July produce a light khaki with alum and an ammonia rinse, but browns with chrome and copper. In Scotland Gypsywort was used to dye yarn for tartan to get a 'lettuce green', this was from fresh leaves in June as the plant starts to grow.

Gypsywort on river bank.

Sample of dyes – gypsywort tops and roots.

HEATHER

(Ling) *Calluna vulgaris*

Calluna comes from the Greek verb 'to sweep': it was used to make brushes. Before hops it was used to make beer, but care needs to be taken as it is prone to an ergot-type fungus that is hallucinogenic. The heather was used in summer when the plant was in flower. There is evidence of its use from Mesolithic sites. It can be grazed by sheep and deer and for feeding red grouse. In Shetland it was used to make rope that was to be used at sea, as salt water does not rot it. Mattresses were stuffed with heather and it was said to be healthy to lie on and had a good scent.

This perennial shrub grows well on very acid soils in both full sun and half shade. It will withstand salt conditions, but it prefers lime-free soils. It could be grown in pots in ericaceous soil. It is an ornamental plant and has a variety of flower colours and leaf forms. The plant regenerates well after burning. It flowers from July to October and the seeds ripen from October to November. It is pollinated by bees, flies, moths, butterflies, and the wind. It can be grown from seed but will need to overwinter for the first year in the greenhouse. Half-ripe cuttings can be taken in July and August and mature wood cuttings in October and November.

Heather can be used at any time of year but it is best when it first starts to bloom. The flowering tops produce yellowy brown with alum, gold with chrome and, if an after-bath of iron is used, a range of greens and greys. When the whole top of the plant is cut up and boiled then orange browns are produced. Traditionally it was used to produce black colour with iron. It was thought that when taken from plants grown in the shade it would produce darker colours.

Shades of orange and brown blend well in Fairisle patterns.

Sample of dyes – heather tops.

HEMP AGRIMONY

Eupatorium cannabinum

Hemp agrimony is known as 'strawberries and cream' because of the pink colour of the flowers. The leaves are used to stop bread from going mouldy. Its leaves are unpalatable to rabbits.

This plant grows in damp conditions often beside streams, up to 2m (6ft 6in) tall. It is not frost tender. The flowers appear from July to September and the seeds ripen from August until October. It is pollinated by insects, bees and butterflies and is self-fertile. The seeds are best sown out in their permanent position from April to June, the seedlings needing to be thinned out to grow 5cm (2in) apart. The plants need to be 30cm (1ft) apart for flowering throughout the following summer. The roots can be divided in spring or autumn.

All the top of the plant is cut up and boiled and it produces a fawn with alum and tin, a light green with chrome and a yellow green with copper. The flowers give a range of good clear yellows.

Hemp agrimony in water meadows.

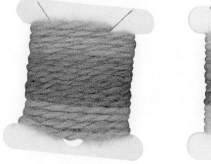

Sample of dyes – hemp agrimony tops and flowers.

HOLLYHOCK

Alcea rosea

There is evidence that the hollyhock was used in Central Asian oases for dyeing silk and skins. It is used as a food colourant. The long stem fibres harvested in the late summer are used for paper-making. The red dye is used in litmus.

Hollyhock is both a hardy annual and a hardy perennial and grows well in temperate climates. It can reach a height of 2m (6ft 6in). It prefers to be sheltered from wind and in a sunny position in rich soil. When mature the plants need to be 90cm (3ft) apart. It can be grown from seed planted in the spring; the perennials are planted in early summer to flower the following summer, from July to September. The seeds ripen from August to October. The leaves are prone to rust and they are attractive to slugs. The modern varieties have some resistance to rust.

The deep red 'black'-flowered varieties give good green dyes. The red-coloured ones give deep oranges. The paler coloured petals give pinky yellows and yellows. The leaves give yellows and lime greens. All have a good light and wash fastness.

Pink hollyhock in garden.

Sample of dyes – hollyhock black flower, deep red flower and pink/yellow flower.

IVY

Hedera helix

The resin in the ivy stems has been used to produce a red dye. The leaves boiled in soda are a soap substitute. Plants grown indoors remove toxins from the atmosphere. This plant tolerates most conditions and will survive atmospheric pollution. As ivy grows well in mild climates, the ivy pollen has been used to date prehistoric climate temperatures.

Ivy is an evergreen climber and comes in many varieties. It will grow from seed and by half-ripe cuttings in July and August and mature wood cuttings in November. The flowers appear from October to November and the seeds from May to June. It is pollinated by bees, flies, moths and butterflies. The berries are poisonous in large quantities and may cause skin irritation, so gloves should be worn when harvesting. The berries are only fully ripe in February – the problem with this is that the birds tend to eat them before the dyer can get to them.

The chopped leaves give deep yellow colours. The ripe berries when mashed give grey-green, but when acid is used in the rinse, give pinky hues. As with most berries the colour is not very light fast. Black is achieved if iron is added to the wool dyed with leaves.

Unripe ivy berries in December.

Sample of dyes – ivy leaves.

Japanese indigo growing in the greenhouse with tomatoes in vermiculite.

JAPANESE INDIGO
Polygonum tinctorium

In Japan the indigo is 'Ai' from the 'Tadeai' plant and written records date back to the seventh century when the raw leaf was used. The fermentation in a vat did not develop until later. It was then used to dye cotton and silk kimonos. The technique was kept secret and was passed down from mother to daughter. The vat was regulated by taste, smell, appearance and feel, so took years to learn and perfect.

This indigo can be grown from seed, needing a long season, so it needs to be started in a greenhouse or cold frame and planted out after late frost, in fertile soil, in full sun and kept well watered. The leaves can be harvested from July onwards. Several crops can be harvested. If some are left to flower they will set seed, which can be used the next year. They will need to be protected from early autumn frosts.

Use un-mordanted yarn unless you want to top dye. Green leaves and stem are crushed and soaked in cold water. You could try liquidizing the leaves with a little water. Bring slowly up to 50°C (120°F) but no higher, as this damages the enzymes, and remove from heat, leaving aside for an hour; then pour off the liquid and squeeze out the leaves to extract juice. The leaf residue can be composted. This sherry-coloured liquid is your dye liquor. Add washing soda or ammonia until it turns green. Aerate the liquid by whisking or by pouring from one container to another. When the froth turns from blue to yellow, it is ready. Put into dye pot and heat up to 50°C (120°F) and sprinkle the powdered reducing agent onto the surface. (This chemical removes the oxygen from the solution.)

Do not stir; leave for fifteen minutes and the bath should now be clear and straw coloured. Add the

Japaneses indigo leaf being liquidized.

wetted yarn, gently submerge and leave for ten minutes, extract carefully, squeeze excess liquid into a separate bowl. Aerate the yarn so that it turns from yellow to blue. Keep dipping until you have achieved the depth of colour required. This is better than a longer dipping time. Rinse, wash in soapy water and rinse again in either salty water or with a few drops of vinegar. To neutralize the vat when the dye is exhausted, whisk to oxygenate and dispose of it in a soakaway. If you treat the leaves as other dye material and boil you will get pinky fawns. If these are then dipped into the indigo bath described above a bright green is obtained.

Japanese indigo plant with yarn sample.

Sample of dyes – Japanese indigo using four dips in the vat, dipped mordanted yarn, boiled leaves and boiled leaves then dipped into indigo vat.

LADY'S BEDSTRAW

(Dyer's bedstraw, Curdwort, Robin in the Hedge, Maiden's hair, Strawbed) *Galium verum*

The Celts used the root to dye their wool red. The soft flowering tops were used to stuff mattresses and had a pleasant scent, which warded away fleas. The leaves and flower contain an enzyme which curdles milk so was used in the cheese-making process. The yellow dye from the tops provided the colour for butter and cheese. The plant is related to madder but does not contain as much colour, and the roots are much finer.

This is a low growing plant with fine stems and clusters of tiny yellow flowers in July and August. The seeds ripen in August and September. Pollination is by flies and beetles and it is self-fertile. It grows in most conditions and will tolerate salt. It is an invasive plant so it may be best to grow it in a deep container. The seeds are best sown *in situ*, in well prepared soil and covered very lightly with fine soil. They can be slow to germinate. Prick out when large enough to handle. Roots can be divided in the spring. The roots are very difficult to harvest and clean. It needs to grow for three years before the roots are worth harvesting as the thinner roots have yellow tones. The Elephant Hawk moth feeds on the plant at night.

To dye one needs 50% root, which has been harvested in the autumn when the tops have died back, then chopped or dried and powdered for later use. The roots are best soaked overnight or longer. The addition of chalk or slaked lime and bran to the dye bath helps the process. The pre-mordanted and wetted wool is added to the bath and the temperature is raised over the course of an hour to no more than 80°C (170°F) for alum, 60°C (120°F) with chrome and 100°C (212°F) with tin. The temperature is kept constantly at these temperatures for two hours then left to cool in the dye bath. If dyeing with the roots, then the bits can be shaken out and readmitted to the dye bath for further dips. The wool is rinsed in hot soapy water. The dye bath seems to improve with use and many shades can be obtained before the dye is exhausted. The red is less strong than the madder and an orangey red is produced.

Lady's bedstraw leaves.

Sample of dyes – lady's bedstraw root.

LILAC

Syringa vulgaris

Lilac is native of the Far East, and was introduced into Britain in the time of Henry VIII. The word *syringa* means hollow tube, and lilac was used to make reed pipes and flutes. Legend has it that this is what Pan's original pipes were made from. The wood from a mature tree is very dense and can be used to make musical instruments and knife handles. Lilac has also been used in the treatment of malaria. It contains essential oils, which are often used in perfumery.

Lilac is a deciduous shrub, from the same the family as the olive, and grows up to 3m (10ft) tall; as a tree, it grows to 7m (23ft). It is a common plant in Britain as it does well in a cool and temperate climate and is often seen in scrubby rocky positions. It prefers limestone and chalk soils. It is a common scented, garden plant and is attractive to butterflies. The flowers in May grow on old wood, so pruning, if necessary, should be done straight after flowering. The original colour of the blossoms was light purple (lilac), but there are now many varieties and the colours range from white, through pink and magenta, to deep purple. A new plant may take several years before it comes into blossom. It suckers freely, and these can be divided and planted out in December and January. It makes a good hedge plant. The lilac needs to be in an airy position, otherwise it is prone to mildew. Cuttings from young shoots or half-ripe wood can be taken in the early summer. The seeds ripen in August. Lilac can be grown from seed sown in March in a cold frame but they will need to be warm stratified for four weeks and cold stratified for three weeks to encourage germination. If the plants are well grown by autumn, they will survive their first winter outside, otherwise you will need to overwinter them in the cold frame and plant them out in spring.

The flowers are cut up and boiled and produce a greeny-yellow colour. The twigs are cut into pieces boiled and left to soak. When dyed, the wool turns to yellow and orange. The spring leaves give vivid yellows and oranges.

Sample of dyes – lilac young leaves and flowers.

MADDER

Rubia tinctorum

Madder leaves with dye sample of root dye.

Madder root is one of the ancient red dyes. There was cotton cloth dyed with madder found in Egypt in Tutankhamen's tomb. Archaeologists have also found traces in the bottom of pottery bowls in old York. Historically it has been used to dye cotton 'Turkey Red' which involves many steps in mordanting. It has been used to dye uniforms of the British Redcoats and hunting 'pink'. It was imported from Flanders and Holland as dried root or as powder and, as a result, by 1750 it was no longer cultivated commercially in England. When synthetic alizarin was made in 1870s the commercial use declined. When used with spirit, it is used as a varnish stain for violins. It was used to dye leather. When madder is fed to birds their beaks and claws turn red; in animals it turns the bones red and this can be used to examine the growth of bone. Historically the juice when beaten out of the roots and leaves has been used to remove freckles and skin blemishes.

This is a hardy perennial that will withstand freezing. It tends to be sprawling and be invasive so should be grown in a large enclosed space; this also helps with the harvesting of the roots. It prefers a light, well-drained soil enriched with sheep manure. It needs to be well drained in winter so that the roots do not rot when dormant. It can be grown from seed: germination is improved if the husk is sandpapered or kept in a refrigerator for a week before it is sown. Root division can also be used as a method of propagation.

Madder can be used to dye many different colours and shades, from pinks, red and lilac to black; when boiled it will give oranges and rich browns. For dyeing, the best roots are three years old, when the outside is a black bark and the inside is red with a yellow core. These can be harvested either before flowering in spring or when the growth has died back in the autumn.

To dye you will need 50% root, either fresh and chopped or dried and powdered. It is best ground and soaked overnight or even for a week before use. The addition of chalk or slaked lime and bran to the dye bath helps the process. The pre-mordanted and wetted wool is added to the bath and the temperature is raised over the course of an hour to no more than 80°C (175°F) for alum, 60°C (140°F) with chrome and 100°C (212°F) with tin. The temperature is kept constantly at these temperatures for two hours then left to cool in the dye bath. If dyeing with the roots, then the bits can be shaken out and readmitted to the dye bath for further dips. After dyeing, the wool is rinsed in hot soapy water. The dye bath seems to improve with use and many shades can be obtained before the dye is exhausted. If alum is used as the pre-mordant, and copper is used after the dyeing, then a good dark maroon is produced. If the temperature is allowed to rise to boiling then orange and brown colours appear.

Sample of dyes – madder root, root exhaust and after-mordanted with copper.

MAHONIA

(Oregon grape) *Mahonia japonica*

The original mahonia plants came from the Far East. Mahonia is a member of the berberis family. It is used in Sikkim for dyeing cotton and silk. Mahonia is poisonous to livestock. The red berries can be eaten, but there is very little flesh around the seed. These have a high vitamin C content. The variety *Mahonia aquifolium* (Oregon grape) is found in North America, and was used by the Native American tribes to dye buckskin, porcupine quills and basket-making materials yellow.

This ornamental evergreen shrub can grow as tall as 3m (10ft), and produces small yellow flowers in April and May and blue-black berries in autumn. It tolerates both drought and humidity, as well as salty conditions, and is insect- and deer-resistant. It can be grown from seed but is best planted after cold stratification and put in the greenhouse for the first winter. The roots can be divided and suckers planted in spring.

The roots and bark are harvested in the autumn. The roots are then cleaned and chopped; they are then soaked for several days before being heated and simmered for an hour. With alum, they give a dark green. The leaves are chopped and left to ferment for a week, give pale green with alum, with chrome a yellowy green, and with copper a dark khaki. The bark, when fermented and mordanted with chrome, gives a brassy yellow; with alum and tin, a dark orange; and with copper a dark khaki. The crushed ripe berries produce a pale purple, which is not light fast.

Sample of dyes – mahonia leaves and stem.

x section x 10

MARIGOLD

Tagetes erecta

Marigolds originated in South America where the Aztecs treated them as sacred flowers. The Spaniards then brought them to Europe. They are used in Hindu ceremonies as garlands to decorate their gods. The petals used to be fed to hens and it gives a yellow colour to the flesh and brightens the yolk of eggs. Its active ingredient is used in modern-day food colouring and is used as a substitute for saffron.

This is a half-hardy annual that does well in high summer temperatures. Marigolds vary in height from the dwarf varieties up to 90cm (3ft). Both African and French varieties can be used for dyeing. The flowering season lasts from June to November. They are pollinated by bees. They grow well in rich, moist soils in full sun but will grow in very acid and very alkaline conditions. The seedlings should be planted out after the risk of frost. They are used near outdoor tomatoes and potatoes as the root secretions keep the white fly away. They do get attacked by slugs and snails, and are susceptible to botrytis. The flowers can be used as a compost activator.

The fresh or dried flowers from all varieties of marigold are simmered in water for an hour with the yarn. The wool with alum and tin gives yellow; with chrome, light tan; and with copper, a green. When combined with blue from either woad or indigo good deep greens are obtained.

Cushion centre, using pale yellows and greens.

Sample of dyes – marigold flowers.

MEADOWSWEET

(Queen of the meadow, Meadwort, Bridewort) *Filipendula ulmaria, Spiraea ulmaria*

This plant has been used to strew on floors at weddings because of its sweet smell. It has been used as one of the main ingredients for mead. The plant contains salicylic acid, which is the active ingredient of aspirin. In the past the flower heads were hung in houses to hide unpleasant smells.

It is a hardy perennial with long fibrous roots. It can be grown from seed in spring or by division of clumps in spring or autumn. Meadowsweet grows up to 1m (3ft) tall in rich moist soils in partial shade. The flowers appear in July and August; as they contain prussic acid, which is very poisonous, it is best not to use them in flower arrangements.

The tops of the whole plant are used and will give yellow with alum and tin. The roots are cut up and soaked overnight in boiling water. The yarn is added to the cold dye bath and slowly brought back up to boiling then simmered for an hour. With alum it gives rose red, with chrome it produces brown, and with copper and iron, black. Leave in the bath until cold and then rinse in warm soapy water.

Meadowsweet in water meadows.

Sample of dyes – meadowsweet tops, roots and roots with iron.

NETTLE

Urtica dioica

This plant has been used to make paper; treated like linen it can be spun and was also used for sail-cloth. Shrouds woven from nettle fibre have been found in a Bronze Age burial site in Denmark. It grows well in soil rich in nitrogen, and therefore is often an indicator of disturbed ground where there are sites of old settlements and houses. The leaves are rich in iron and Vitamin C. Young leaves are often used in soups. It has been used as a hair conditioner and is supposed to promote hair growth. In Ukraine it is used to dye Easter eggs and as a green dye in confectionery. Extract from the leaves is used as a fertilizer. The juice from the leaves was used to seal leaking wooden barrels as it coagulates and seals the joints. Nettle leaves were used to line the boxes of fruit going to the London markets to assist the ripening. Even today some cheeses are wrapped in the leaves.

This perennial is readily available and grows to 1.5m (5ft). It contains formic acid, which explains why it stings if touched: gloves should be used if picking the leaves. When cooked it loses its sting. It begins to grow in March, flowers from May to October and sets seed from June to October. It is pollinated by the wind. It is grown by root division or by seed. Nettles attract many insect and butter-flies such as Red Admiral, Comma, Peacock, Painted Lady and Small Tortoiseshell; their caterpillars eat the leaves.

The fresh tops in spring are simmered for one hour and cooled, at which point the liquid can be strained and used. If simmered for one hour with the wool it gives a yellow colour but when simmered for two hours with the leaves and left to cool in the dye bath, the iron present in the leaves has the effect of producing greens. The residue of the leaves makes good compost. The cut up roots boiled with salt and alum produce a yellow.

Nettle patch.

Sample of dyes – nettle tops and tops soaked for twenty-four hours.

OAK

Quercus robur

Oak wood resists rotting and has been used to build boats, furniture and houses. It also makes good firewood. The acorns have been fed to pigs. The dye, combined with gum arabic and iron, is used to make black ink. The oak bark and galls (growths produced by fungi and insects) were used to tan leather. As a mordant it is used on silk to give it weight.

The mature oak tree grows from an acorn to a tree up to 25m (80ft) tall. It is slow-growing and often found as an isolated specimen. It tolerates a wide range of conditions but does not do well in shallow soils or in salt air. It is resistant to honey fungus. The flowers appear in April and May and the acorns in September and October. It is pollinated by the wind. It has an extremely high wildlife value, particularly for insects. The gall wasp lays its eggs in the oak buds. This encourages growth, which swells around the grub to form a sphere that hardens. When the grub is mature it leaves by a small hole. If you plant acorns be aware that mice and squirrels will eat them. As seedlings grow a tap root they do not transplant well, so acorns are better planted *in situ*.

Oak bark and galls can be used as a mordant. Soak the oak galls and the stripped bark for a week then boil for an hour. The oak galls with alum-mordanted wool give yellow, and with iron, black. The bark after a week of soaking gives yellows, oranges and tan. The leaves when torn up and boiled with copper give shades of brown. Do not prolong the dyeing with bark, as the tannins will tend to dull the colour.

Oak galls.

Sample of dyes – oak leaves and bark.

ONION

Allium

Onions are thought to have originated in Asia but they are widespread. They have been a valuable food source as they store well and give flavour to food. In Egypt they were worshipped because of their circular shape. The juice is used to prevent rust on metals, and to polish brass and copper. If rubbed on the skin it acts as an insect repellent.

This is a hardy perennial. It grows well in deeply dug well-drained soil in full sun. It flowers from June to July and is pollinated by bees and insects. The seeds are sown in early spring or by planting sets.

The skins can be stored as the onions are peeled in the kitchen but must be kept dry to prevent them from going mouldy. The nylon net bags from the vegetable shops are ideal for keeping the skins aired. Red-skinned onions with wool give gold with alum and tin, reddish gold with chrome and tan brown with copper. When used on cotton with chrome the colour is a dark tan. Yellow-skinned onions give yellow with alum, brassy yellow with chrome and a bright yellow with tin. All these have a good light and wash fastness. It is possible to dye with onion skins without mordants but the colours are less light fast and paler. However, avoiding the use of chemicals is good if working with children.

A dye bath with onion skins and unmordanted yarn.

Sample of dyes – yellow-skinned and red-skinned onion.

PERFORATED ST JOHN'S WORT
Hypericum perforatum

Historically this plant was gathered on St John's Eve, 23 June. It was used by bakers to improve the texture of the bread. Medicinally, it is widely used as an antidepressant. The sap is poisonous to animals as it produces a photo-toxic reaction after being eaten. The red sap from the leaves was thought to represent the blood of St John the Baptist. The devil was supposed to hate the plant so much that he stuck needles into the leaves to destroy it, hence the tiny holes. A spray of the plant was thought to protect against witches and the devil, and the house from fire, thunder and lightning.

This plant grows from tubers and the small lanceolate (tapered) leaves have tiny holes, which can be seen when held up to the light. It grows to 30cm (1ft). It blooms from June to August and sets seed July to September. It is pollinated by bees and flies and is self-fertile. It needs a well-drained soil and will tolerate drought; it is best grown in full sun. It tends to grow wild in semi-shade and along field margins. It can be grown from seed but can take up to three months to germinate. The roots can be divided in September and October.

The tops of the plant boiled up in water will produce a variety of yellows. If just the flowers are used, then with vinegar the colours take a reddish tinge. If an alcoholic extraction, which produces a clear red solution, is used then it will produce violet-red on both silk and wool when rinsed in vinegar. The colours produced vary through the seasons.

Perforated St Johns wort plant.

Perforated St Johns wort steeping in alcohol.

Sample of dyes – perforated St Johns wort flowers in water and flowers in spirit.

POT MARJORAM

Origanum marjorana, Labiatae origanuum,
Marjorana hortensis

Marjoram is indigenous to the Mediterranean region. It was grown in herb gardens and used in cooking and herbal remedies. Its sweet odour led it to be used as a deodorant and as a preservative. A perfume can be made from the roots. The herb is used in egg and cheese dishes, soups and fish dishes. It was used to scent winding sheets, and frequently it was planted on the grave.

This perennial shrub grows 10–40cm (4–16in) tall. It is not frost-hardy. Marjoram flowers from June to September and the seeds ripen in August and September. It is pollinated by bees. It will tolerate most conditions but prefers slightly alkaline soils. It grows on dry slopes and in rocky places but will tolerate shade. The seeds germinate in two to four weeks and seedlings can then be potted on and moved to their permanent positions in early summer. Roots can be divided in spring or autumn. It is attractive to bees and butterflies such as the caterpillar of the Common Blue butterfly.

The whole of the tops are cut up and boiled to give greens. If just the flowers are used, with alum and tin they give gold and tan; with chrome they give tan. The tops dye cotton cloth purple, and linen reddish brown.

Pot marjoram flowers.

Sample of dyes – pot marjoram tops and flowers and just flowers.

PRIVET

Ligustrum vulgare

The privet is a native of Europe and Asia. It is used for hedging and topiary. The wood is a creamy white and when polished looks like bone.

Privet is a hardy perennial growing to a height of 3m (10ft) if not pruned. It likes a well-drained soil in the sun or partial shade. It is tolerant of atmospheric pollution and salt winds but is susceptible to honey fungus. It flowers in June and July and the seeds are ripe from September and October. It is pollinated by insects. It can be grown from seed or by half-ripe wood cuttings taken in July and August and mature wood cuttings in November and December. Harvest leaves in early summer until the first frosts, and the ripe berries in the Autumn. The Privet Hawk moth caterpillar eats the leaves.

The fresh leaves produce bright yellow with alum, gold with chrome and a dark green with iron. All these give good light and wash fastness. Berries gathered in September have a poor fastness and are poisonous. They give lilacs and purples and, with acid rinse, turn pink.

Sample of dyes – privet leaves.

Privet hedge and sample of dyed yarn.

RAGWORT

(St James's wort, Stinking willy) *Senecio jacobaea, Senecio squalidus*

This contains poisonous alkaloids, which affect the liver. The cinnabar caterpillars that eat the leaves are thought to benefit from this as it makes them unpalatable to predators. It is defined as a 'noxious' weed in the 1959 Weed Act in Britain (www.ragwortfacts.info/html) but its removal is not enforced. It is poisonous to horses but sheep can safely eat small quantities and it is thought to kill their stomach worms. When cut and wilted it looses its bitterness and becomes palatable but is still poisonous, so ragwort must not be left in the field after pulling.

This is a hardy perennial and grows to 90cm (3ft) tall. It flowers from June to October and sets seed from July to October. It is pollinated by bees, flies, moths and butterflies and is self-fertile. It thrives on poor soil and full sun and it is an invasive weed. The flower heads should be removed so that the seeds cannot spread. The milky juice can cause an allergic reaction so rubber gloves must be worn.

Use both leaves and stems cut up. With alum it produces a green but this fades to pale greeny fawn. The flowers in summer give rich yellows with alum, an orange-yellow with chrome, and orange with tin. The residue of the plant material can be composted.

Ragwort flowers.

Sample of dyes – ragwort whole tops and flowers.

RHUBARB

Rheum rhabarbarum

In China rhubarb has been used as medicine and the first record of its use is in 2700BC. Marco Polo referred to it so it may have come to Europe via Venice. Rhubarb is a native plant of Mongolia where it has been used to dye wool for their rugs. It is the principal dye used by Tibetans and with madder produces a good orange. In Turkestan it is used to tan leather.

This plant is hardy and frost resistant. It grows on well-drained moist loam or clay. It is immune to rabbits. It dies back in autumn but grows from the crown the following spring. It is mostly grown by division of the crown but can be grown from seed. These must be planted in a cold frame, grown on in their first year, over-wintered in a frost-free place then planted out the following spring. The root is used either fresh or powdered, collected in spring or autumn. When collecting the stems, they should be pulled and twisted so that they come away clean from the crown. Leave at least three stalks to allow the plant to continue to grow.

The leaves are rich in oxalic acid and are used as a mordant. Cut into small pieces and add water, bring to the boil and simmer for an hour. 1kg (2lb) of leaves will be enough to mordant about 3kg (6lb) of wool. When mordanting fibres do so in a well-ventilated space and wear a mask when working with the bath, as the fumes are toxic. When dyeing with alum it produces an orange with good fastness. When washing soda is added it turns to red or coral pink, and with iron will give an olive green.

Overwintering rhubarb.

Sample of dyes – rhubarb leaves (with no mordant at top with Al, Cr, Cu, Sn) and roots.

SAFFLOWER

(False Saffron) *Carthamus tinctorius*

The safflower comes from Egypt and the Middle East and is still cultivated in the Mediterranean regions and commercially in France. The Egyptians used it to dye the bands they used for mummification. It is used as pigment for paint and cosmetics. The dye is not colour fast and is used on cotton to produce 'red tape' for legal documents: if they are untied then it is possible to see that they have been tampered with as it is difficult to retie the tape in the same place. It is also used to colour rice. The oil is used as a diesel substitute and has been used to waterproof cloth. When the colour is extracted with alcohol and mixed with talcum powder it is used as rouge. Safflower is also known as 'false saffron' and was used to bulk out saffron, but it is not as good.

It is a hardy annual or biannual and grows to 1m (3ft) high. It can tolerate very dry conditions and full sun but needs a long, hot growing season. If the growing season is too short, seeds will not be produced. It forms a rosette of leaves. As it is a spiky plant it is best not to plant it adjacent to paths in the garden. It grows from seed sown in early spring in a greenhouse and germinates quickly but does not transplant well so it should be started in individual plant containers, gradually hardened off, and planted out from the end of May. Safflower does well in dry, un-manured soils.

The flowers are picked in June and July in the morning after the dew has dried or in the evening at sundown. Flowers picked at sundown and used fresh are better than dried heads. The flowers can be used with alum to give a clear yellow, with tin a rust colour and when iron is added, brass. It is an excellent dye on silk, which is a bright yellow when mordanted. When yellow is washed out, it will give rose to scarlet. In Japan the petals are dried and made into 'cakes'.

To remove the yellow colour, the petals are put into a cotton bag with cold water and vinegar, left to soak for a few hours, then squeezed out until the water becomes clear. The petals are then rinsed and covered with cold water and small amount of washing soda. When squeezed out the red liquor can be neutralized with vinegar. Heat liquid to no more than 65°C (150°F) and put the yarn in for two hours, then use a vinegar rinse. It produces reds and oranges on silk and cotton.

Safflower flower.

Sample of dyes – safflower leaves and stalk and flower head with yellow washed out wool, cotton and silk.

SAFFRON
Crocus sativus

Saffron, the spice derived from the dried stigma of the crocus flower, has been cultivated for at least 4,000 years. It is grown commercially in the Mediterranean countries. In England the area around Saffron Walden used to be the centre for cultivation. In Medieval times it was used as a hair dye. Monks mixed it with egg white to produce a golden yellow that was used in their illuminated manuscripts. It is used on cotton for Buddhists' robes, and was also used for the bright yellows and oranges in Persian carpets. In Marseilles, the bouillabaisse, a thick soup made from several different kinds of fish, uses saffron.

It is very costly to produce: it takes approximately 60,000 stigmas (each crocus has three stigmas) to make 450g (1lb) of dried saffron and when grown commercially an acre of ground could produce just 1.8kg (4lb) of saffron stigmas.

The soil should be rich, well worked, and with good drainage. Saffron needs a hot sunny position, sheltered from wind and frost. The corms should be planted about 15cm (6in) apart at a depth two and a half times the size of the corm. Summer is the best time to plant out. As the corms last for up to fifteen years and have a tendency to work their way lower into the soil each year, they should be lifted every three years, to be split and replanted. The leaves appear from October to May and it flowers in October. It is pollinated by bees and butterflies. Each bulb will produce two or three lilac flowers

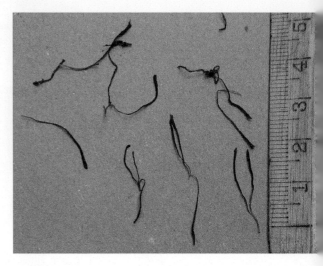

Dried saffron stigmas.

each autumn. The leaves are fine and grass-like and die back in the summer. The plants can be propagated by dividing the bulbs when they are dormant in the summer.

The stigmas are gathered in the early morning in September or October. They are about 2.5cm (1in) long and a bright orangey red. Birds tend to be attracted to them and peck at them, so some form of mesh above might prevent this. Once picked, they should be dried immediately. It is a powerful dye so you do not need much. It can be used on wool either unmordanted or mordanted to produce a range of yellows and golds. The flower petals produce a blue-green colour.

Sample of dyes – saffron stigmas on wool and stigmas on cotton and silk.

Sally Pinhey

SOAPWORT

(Bouncing Betty, Fuller's herb) *Saponaria officinalis*

Used in Roman times as a cleaning agent, soapwort is still used by conservators to clean delicate fabrics. It was used to clean the Bayeaux Tapestry.

This perennial is grown from creeping root stock and is very invasive. It grows well in damp friable soils up to 75cm (2ft 6in) tall. The flowers appear from July to September and it sets seed in August and September. It is pollinated by moths and butterflies. It can be propagated by division. The seeds take up to a month to germinate. Plant out after the risk of late frosts. It attracts moths and butterflies.

It is poisonous to fish so do not plant near ponds or water courses.

The best time to harvest the tops is in midsummer and for the roots (which contain most of the saponins, the active ingredient) spring or autumn. Both leaves and roots are put in cold water and brought to the boil. The liquor is then strained off. This does not produce much lather but does clean without damaging the fibre. It loses its effectiveness in a couple of days so a new solution needs to be made just before use. It will not clean thick grease but is effective for fragile fabrics and lightly stained items. When the whole top of the plant is used for dyeing, it produces pale greens. If only the flowers are used then the colours are pale yellows and greens.

Soapwort flowers.

Soapwort bath with soap bubbles.

Sample of dyes – soapwort tops and flowers.

SORREL

(French sorrel) *Rumex acetosa, Rumex scutatus*

Sorrel is a native of Asia and Europe. The word sorrel is thought to have been derived from the French word *surele*, where *sur* means sour. The 'sour grass' was made into a sauce, which was eaten with cold fatty meats such as pork, mutton and goose. The leaves are rich in Vitamin C and were used to combat scurvy on long sea voyages. It is also used in herbal medicines as a laxative. It contains high levels of oxalic acid, which is reduced when cooked. It is not good for people with rheumatism or arthritis. The juice from the leaves is used as a curdling agent for milk and is used to remove stains from linen.

This perennial herb has arrow-shaped edible leaves, which change colour from bright green in spring to a crimson-red in late summer. The flowering spikes, which appear from May to July, change from a greeny-red to purple as they mature. It grows up to 50cm (1ft 6in) tall. It has a deep juicy root stem. Cutting the leaves encourages further growth.

The seeds can be planted in open ground. Sorrel prefers rich, moisture-retentive soil, either in full sun or partial shade. The seedlings need to be thinned out to 5cm (2in) apart. In the autumn the spacing needs to be 30cm (1ft) for flowering the following summer. The plants produce leaves within eight weeks. The roots can be divided at any time of the year. Unfortunately the slugs and snails are attracted to the leaves, so the young plants will need to be protected.

The best colour for dyeing is obtained from fresh spring leaves. Older leaves, when chopped and boiled, give very pale colours except when used with tin when a bright yellow is obtained. The roots produce orangey browns. The roots can be used as a mordant as they have a high oxalic acid content. The roots need to be washed to remove any soil, then cut into small pieces. As oxalic acid is poisonous, wear gloves when handling and cutting up sorrel. Cover the roots with water and simmer for an hour. Keep a lid on the pan and avoid breathing the fumes and make sure the place where you are dyeing is well-ventilated. The liquid is then strained and can be used as a mordant bath for wool or silk. The quantity used is about half the weight dry wool to dry weight of root. The amount may vary as to the type of sorrel used, growing conditions, and the age and size of the root. It will colour the yarn yellow, so will affect the shade of colour obtained when used in a dye bath using a different plant.

Sample of dyes – sorrel leaves and roots.

TANSY

(Bachelor's buttons, Bitter buttons, Cow bitter) *Tanacetum vulgare*

Tansy is a native of Asia. It is a medicinal herb that is toxic to internal parasites and is therefore used as a vermifuge. It has a pungent smell and was rubbed on meat because it warded off flies. The sprays were used as a strewing herb and to keep moths away. When planted amongst fruit trees tansy is said to keep away fruit tree moths. The name *Tanacetum* is derived from the Greek word *athanasia*, which means immortality: the flowers do not wilt when picked and it was packed into coffins with the corpse to preserve it. As it was thought to be a disinfectant it was used in the streets during the Great Plague.

The tansy is a hardy perennial and grows in clumps about 50cm (1ft 6in) tall. It is tolerant of a variety of soil conditions. It will grow in full sun or shade. The leaves start growing in April and the flowers appear in June to September and it sets seeds from August to October. It is pollinated by bees, flies and beetles and is self-fertile. It grows from roots and seeds and is invasive. It is often found on waste ground. It can be grown from seed or by root division in the spring. The tops are rich in potassium and can be added to the compost heap. It is often used as a companion plant to cucumbers, squashes and roses as it repels the beetles and ants.

The dye bath has a pungent smell so dyeing is best done outside or in a well-ventilated room. The chopped leaves and flowers in equal weight to the fibres are brought to the simmer in an hour, and then simmered for another hour. This gives a variety of yellows and yellow-greens with the different mordants. The fresh young leaves in the spring produce an acid lemon, green and tan.

Tansy plants.

Sample of dyes – tansy leaves and flowers.

WALLFLOWER
Erysimum cheiri

The wallflower is a native plant of Morocco. In Medieval times, wallflowers were planted in gardens because their scent masked the smell of poor drains. In Elizabethan times, the wallflower was commonly known as a gillyflower and was carried as one of the flowers in a nosegay. These sweet-smelling posies were thought to ward off common diseases. The Old English word *cherisaunce* means comfort and was applied to flowers carried in important ceremonies such as weddings. The wallflower is frequently used as a bedding plant in public parks. The essential oil is used in perfumery.

The wild variety of wallflower has only small orangey yellow flowers, whereas the cultivated garden type comes in a range of colours from deep red to strong orange. It is a perennial herb of the cabbage family, and grows to 20cm to 60cm tall with a woody stem. It will grow in mortar joints in walls, although the woody roots are rather prone to breaking off. It flowers from April to June and is pollinated by bees and flies. It prefers a neutral to alkaline soil in full sun. It will tolerate salt atmosphere. The seeds are sown in spring and take up to three weeks to germinate and can be moved to their permanent position in the early summer. The seedlings need to be protected against slugs. If drainage is poor, then the plant tends to turn yellow and rot at the roots. If left to flower and develop seeds, it will self-sow providing the soil conditions are suitable.

The flowering tops, when cut up and boiled with the wool, will give pale greens. These do not have a good light-fastness, and the green will eventually change to a pale yellow. If an iron after-bath is used, then the greens are more permanent.

Sample of dyes – wallflower flowers.

WALNUT

Juglans nigra

Historically it is the husk that has been used to produce a good brown and black. It was used for dyeing the uniforms of the Confederate forces in the American Civil War; the soldiers were nicknamed 'butternuts' due to their deep yellow uniforms. It is also used as a hair dye. Its dark-coloured wood has strong figuring and is used by cabinet makers, turners and wood carvers. Ripe walnuts are eaten and unripe green walnuts pickled. Walnut oil is extracted for culinary purposes. The juice is supposed to keep bed bugs away.

Walnut is a hardy deciduous tree that grows to 15m (5ft) tall and is not suitable for small gardens. It can be susceptible to frost. It does best on loams, chalk and limestone. It flowers from May to June and the nuts ripen in September and October. It is wind pollinated and is self-fertile. The nuts need to be protected against mice, squirrels and birds. Once germinated the seedlings will need to be planted into their permanent positions and protected against frost and cold winds. Pruning should be undertaken in late summer or when the tree is fully dormant, otherwise the cut will bleed and weaken the tree.

Walnut is a substantive dye: it does not require a mordant, but if they are used, it will produce a greater variety of browns and be more permanent. Leaves can be used at the beginning of summer to give yellow. They should be torn apart and soaked for a day before use. Flesh of fruit when covered with water and fermented, and the dye bath kept at 80°C (175°F) for one hour gives a green grey. The green husks are first soaked in hot water overnight or for several days to produce dark browns and with iron will give black. To use bark, pour boiling water over the chopped up bark and leave to soak for a week. To dye, add the fibres and heat the bath gently to 60°C (140°F), keep at that temperature for an hour then leave to cool. This will give a variety of browns. If the bark or husks are to be soaked for a long time, a small amount of white vinegar will inhibit mould growth. The dye is likely to stain anything it comes into contact with and can be used to colour wood and leather. The dried walnut hulls seem to be more potent than the fresh ones. Store the green hulls in the dark as these give a darker dye.

Sample of dyes – walnut new leaves, old leaves, husks and soaked husks.

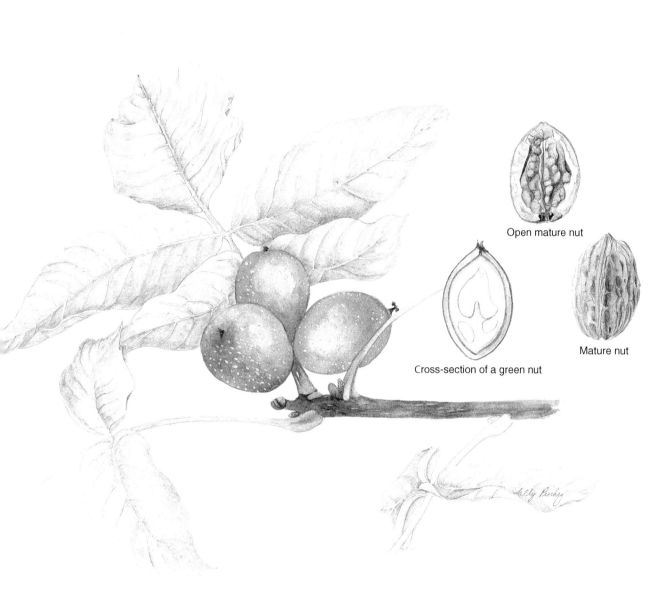

Open mature nut

Cross-section of a green nut

Mature nut

Sally Pinhey

WELD

(Dyer's Rocket, Greenweed, Yellow weed)
Reseda luteola

The weld is a native of the Mediterranean and Southwest Asia. There is evidence of it being used in Neolithic times. The Romans used it to dye the tunics of the vestal virgins. There are records of it being imported into Britain in the Middle Ages.

Weld flowers will turn to face towards the sun even on a cloudy day. It is a herbaceous biennial which grows as a rosette in the first year and a long spike of up to 1.5m (5ft) in the second year. It prefers light soils but will grow on dry sandy and calcareous soils at the side of roads and railway lines. It is found wild in all regions of Europe and on waste ground beside roads. The plant can be grown from seed and once it is established will self-seed and this seems to be the best way of propagation. Sow the seeds in February or March when the soil has warmed up, where you want them to grow as they do not transplant well, because they have long tap roots. If only partially cut the plant will grow side shoots that can be used later. It can be used when dried. It flowers from June to August and sets seed in August and September. It is pollinated by bees and insects and is self-fertile.

The seed has the highest concentration of dye colour. The whole plant is used at a rate of equal weight of dyestuff to yarn. With alum mordant it gives good vibrant lemon yellows with wool, silk, linen and cotton. The chrome produces tans and the copper a brassy colour. Used with madder it gives a good orange and with woad produces Lincoln green and Saxon green.

1) Weld rosette in first year; 2) Weld spike in second year; 3) Weld in flower with yarn sample; 4) Chopped up weld in dye bath; 5) Weld dye on different fibres with different mordants.

Sample of dyes – weld tops, concentrated tops and weld/indigo.

flower x 5

WILLOW

Salix nigra, Salix alba

The light-coloured wood splits easily and is used to make cricket bats because it will withstand compression. The thin stems are used to weave baskets; pollarded willows are used to make hurdles. The wood is used to make charcoal. The bark is used to make a red-brown paper. The roots help to stabilize riverbanks. It will tolerate pollution and coastal winds. The bark contains salicylic acid and was used for aspirin before it was synthesized chemically.

The willow is found throughout Northern Europe and there are many species. It grows easily from cuttings planted 5m (6ft 6in) apart and can become rather invasive, so do not plant close to buildings or drains. The catkins are attractive to insects and bees.

The inner bark, from old wood gathered early in the year, is soaked for several weeks and gives a golden tan with tin and a rose tan with alum. The willow roots give a bluish red colour. Young twigs collected in midsummer give tan with alum. The leaves produce a bright yellow with alum, orange with chrome and tan brown with copper. The wood and bark contain tannins, which act as a mordant, and the colour is a peachy brown.

Mature willow trees.

Sample of dyes – sallow willow leaves, crack willow leaves and willow bark.

WOAD

Isatis tinctoria

This plant has been used for over 2,000 years to produce blue. In Medieval times it was the second most significant import after wine. It has been known for its antibiotic properties and has been used to relieve swollen glands, but is not for internal use. It was last commercially cultivated in Lincolnshire around 1930, when it was used to dye Metropolitan police uniforms. A recent EU sponsored project, Spindigo, has been investigating woad as a source of indigo to replace the synthetic oil-based one. Woad is found in northern Europe and around the Fens of Cambridgeshire. It was the chief source of blue before indigo was imported from the Far East from 1600. It exhausts the soil, so this is why it was cultivated by itinerant growers. As the process used urine and involved a fermentation process it was a very smelly operation and not appreciated by neighbours down wind. The honey made by bees feeding on woad had an unpleasant taste.

It grows well in calcareous rich soils in full sun. Woad is a biennial, growing as a rosette in the first year and producing a stalk up to 1.5m (4ft 3in) tall in the second year. Twenty months after germination, the flowers appear from June to August, and the bunches of black ripe seed hang from the tall arching stems in August and September. The seeds are sown outside in spring and summer and need to be kept well watered. The seedlings can be transplanted when large enough. Woad is pollinated by insects. The leaves can be harvested several times at the rosette stage from the first spring onwards.

Since it is a plant that exhausts the soil, the crop is moved every two years.

No mordant is required unless you need to top dye with yellow to produce greens, and reds to produce maroons and purples. The latest thinking on the best way to extract the dye has been suggested by Dr David Hill: pick leaves in the first year whilst the plant is at the rosette stage (up to five crops can be harvested in the first year). Put them straight into the freezer. This helps to break down the plant material and makes the process more efficient. Chop and shred the leaves and pour on boiling water to scald, press and exclude air; put on a lid and leave for an hour, squeeze to extract brown liquid. Put the liquid into dye bath, heat to no more than 60°C (140°F) and add washing soda or ammonia until liquid turns green. Whisk to aerate until the froth turns from blue to yellow. Add powdered de-oxygenator (sodium metabisulphite or powdered colour run remover). Leave for 15 minutes and it is ready to use. Gently introduce the wetted yarn, leave for 15 minutes, then withdraw without dripping and adding oxygen. Squeeze any excess liquid into a bowl, and aerate the hank. The yellow colour will gradually turn blue as the oxygen reaches the fibres. If a deep blue is required then it is better to build up the colour with several dips. As the vat becomes exhausted then paler blues are obtained. This is a good time to dye the blues to follow with a top dye of yellow to get greens. When the desired colour is achieved, the yarn should be rinsed thoroughly to remove the loose dye, washed in warm soapy water and rinsed in a vinegar solution to counter the strong alkali in the woad vat.

Sample of dyes – woad first, second and third dips on unmordanted yarn.

WOOD AVENS

(Herb bennet, Cloveroot) *Geum urbanum*

The name 'herb bennet' came from the corruption of *Herba Benedicta*, the Blessed Herb. The root has been used as an amulet to ward off evil spirits. The roots have a clove-like scent and flavour and were used in liquor.

It grows in hedges and woodlands in moist rich soil in shady conditions, reaching a height of up to 60cm (2ft) tall. The flowers appear in May and last until August. The freshly dug root smells like clove. The roots are dug and dried. The plant can be grown from seed: in nature the burrs are caught on animal fur and dispersed. It is self-fertile. It grows best when self-sown. Large clumps can be split and transplanted. The dried roots are used to discourage moths and to give a pleasing smell to linen.

If the tops are used to dye, then with alum and tin a pale yellow is produced; with chrome a light green; and with copper a dark gold.

Wood avens plant.

Sample of dyes – wood avens tops.

YELLOW IRIS

(Yellow flag) *Iris pseudacorus*

The fleur-de-lys design was based on the shape of the yellow iris. It is the emblem of the Scout movement. It was used in the Harris tweed for the greens and yellows. The leaves were used to thatch houses. When well roasted and ground the rhizomes have been used as a coffee substitute.

This perennial grows well in marshy ground in full sun up to a height of 90 cm (3ft). The flowers appear between May and August. It is pollinated by bees and hoverflies and is self-fertile. It grows from rhizomes or seed. If growing in peat the rhizomes are easy to dig up. These are best in spring and autumn when the leaves have not yet emerged or in autumn after the leaves have died. This is also a good time to transplant.

As the leaves and rhizomes contain a skin irritant, it is advisable to wear rubber gloves when handling the plant material and the dyed fibres, until well rinsed. The root is washed to remove any soil then cut into small pieces. These are then placed in water and brought to the boil. The yarn can be put in with the dye material, as it is easy to shake out. Once the dark brown colour is achieved, then dip in an iron solution to make the black shades. When less root is used and without the iron then the colour in spring is pink but, with more time in the dye bath, the yarn colour turns to warm brown. The flowers, with alum, give a yellow and the leaves a bright yellow-green.

Yellow iris in water meadow.

Sample of dyes – yellow iris leaves, roots, soaked roots and soaked roots plus iron.

YEW

Taxus baccata

The word *taxus* comes from the Greek meaning 'bow'. The toxins from yew are used to poison the tips of arrows. Most yews grow in churchyards and often pre-date the church, as the yew was worshipped by pre-Christians and many churches were built in sacred places. The slow growth makes it dense and is therefore commonly used for furniture, and its 'elastic' property makes it good for archery bows. For outside use it is very durable.

Yew grows in well-drained chalk soils. It is very long lived and can grow to a large girth size. It is poisonous to animals. Alkaloids, which are heart depressants, are present in the leaves, bark and seeds. The seed covering is not poisonous. It can be grown from seed but is very slow growing. It can withstand a polluted atmosphere and clipping as for a hedge, and it is used for topiary. It will grow in both full sun and in the shade. The flowers appear in March and April, the fruit from September to November. It is pollinated by the wind.

Fresh heartwood chips produce pink, orange and tan. Yew leaves when chopped up and boiled give orange-tans and browns.

Yew hedge.

Different colours obtained from yew wood dye.

Sample of dyes – yew leaves and core wood.

CHAPTER 5

Drying and using plant material

General points

It is useful to be able to dry dye plants for later use. The plant needs to be thoroughly dried, otherwise you will find that it will rot and grow fungus. It is best to spread the material thinly so that the air can circulate on a slatted or mesh rack or an open net or, if possible, tied in bunches and hung upside down in an airy place. A picture frame with net stretched across is a good solution. A clear labelling system is advisable, which notes the name of the plant, the date gathered, the weight when gathered and, if collected from the countryside, where it was growing so that you can revisit and pick some more next year. Also the same plant may be growing in different conditions and therefore give a different shade of colour. You may be able to gather seed as the flower heads dry out.

Flowers

Certain flowers such as Coreopsis will grow more blooms through the season as they are harvested, so it is possible to accumulate enough heads to dye a

Dried hollyhock, coreopsis and dyer's chamomile flowers.

reasonable weight of fibre from a few plants. When totally dried the plant can be cut or broken up into smaller pieces and stored in paper bags or cardboard boxes. (If plastic bags and containers are used then the plant tends to sweat and grow mould.) These need to be stored in a cool, dry place, preferably away from bright sunshine. Flowers are best collected when they are in full bloom and because they tend to be thick and succulent care must be taken to make sure they are dry before storage.

Leaves

These can be fragile when dried and will tend to crumble, so small cardboard boxes are most suitable for storage.

Bark

This is best gathered as the sap is rising in the spring. It should never be taken from a living tree, so fallen branches and sawmills are the best source. As many barks look similar, attention needs to be paid to correct identification and secure labelling of the samples.

Roots

Roots such as madder should be well washed to remove all the earth. It is easier to cut roots into small pieces when fresh than when they are hard and dry. The dried roots can then be put into a coffee grinder just before use. The inner core contains the most dye and so you may be able to strip the outer bark off before drying.

Wood

This is best chipped before storage. If the recipe specifies heartwood or sapwood these need to be separated and labelled.

Skins

Skins such as those of onions, which you may be accumulating over time, need to be dried as you start collecting otherwise you will find a rotten mass at the bottom of the bag. Perhaps a plastic net bag such as those used to deliver carrots and onions to vegetable shops would help keep the skins dry.

Fruits

Those such as berries can be dried but you might like to consider freezing them. If you can liquidize and then dry them, they will be even more ready for the dyeing process, though this sometimes leads to little pieces getting into the yarn that are difficult to separate.

Shells and husks

Those such as walnuts keep well but before use need to be soaked for as long as possible.

Using dried material

All dried material except bark and wood can be used as fresh. If you are making note of the quantities of yarn to dye then use the 'fresh' weight of the dried plant or simply use half as much as you would if they were fresh.

Storing dye plants

The other way to store dyes is to make a liquor. Simply boil the dye material straight after gathering, then decant the liquid into a suitably labelled and dated container. These need to be dark glass or stored in a dark place. Plastic milk containers are readily available but take care that they do not melt when too hot a liquid is poured in. If using soft drinks bottles, please keep these out of the reach of children and make sure that clear labels written with non-fading ink are firmly attached.

LEFT: *Dried weld*   RIGHT: *Onion skins in netting.*

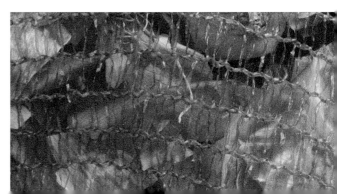

CHAPTER 6

Dye plant gardens

This chapter gives some ideas of how and where dye plants can be grown in your own garden. Illustrations of five different garden plans are included: the main dyer's garden; a front garden; wet and dry gardens; and finally a container garden. Suggested plants are numbered or lettered for each garden. Some dye plants are quite specialist and will not be found easily in hedgerows or on common land. Your own garden is the most convenient place to harvest them. It is not suggested that you sow weed plants such as nettles or dock, which are readily available elsewhere and would be a real nuisance in your garden. While the illustrations show the common plant, in some species the dye-giving properties are also contained in better garden varieties, and where suitable these are suggested. Cultivation advice on root containment and seedlings in the main garden also applies to other gardens.

MAIN GARDEN
6m × 9m (20ft × 30ft)

The orientation of the dyer's garden is not critical and it can easily be adapted to suit specific sites. On this plan the near view from the house is of the flowers around the recreation area and the long view is between the trees to the beehive compost bin. The silver birch (22) provides a feature and in the winter the contrast of the light bark will show up against the dark of the privet hedge (17). Bird feeders can hang in the tree. The change in levels will lead the eye down the garden. The gravel combines simplicity and flexibility of design with unity and ease of maintenance.

The garden is intended to be inexpensive to establish. The main landscaping could be done in one day with a miniature digger, by levelling the central area, putting the excess topsoil where the beds will be and digging the trenches for the brick edges. Two courses of bricks above the level ground are recommended but not essential. The main expenses will be:

- the circular paving which defines the space in the garden throughout the year;
- the beehive compost bin, which takes the eye down the garden;
- the barrel for the water feature; and
- the hurdle fencing, which screens the boundaries and complements the natural wild aspect of the garden.

The table and chairs and garden shed are optional but the cold frame is essential for raising the Japanese indigo (11) and safflower, if used, which need a long growing season. Plants grown for dyeing are different to garden varieties. Many are wild and have a vigorous if not rampant growing habit. The design of the garden reflects this need to contain the plants and make for easy digging and lifting.

The brick edging to the beds should go down 30cm (1ft) below the level of the gravel, to minimize root encroachment into the gravel, and to make the beds easier to tend. Consider concrete footings to the edges. In particular the madder bed (12) should be lined with slates to a depth of 45cm (18in). Madder roots need to be at least two years old, so they will become well established before they are big enough be used for dyeing.

Planting list for main garden

1. Barberry, *Berberis darwini*
2. Blackberry, *Rubus fruticosus*
3. Coreopsis, *Calliopsis tinctoria*
4. Dahlia, *Dahlia variabilis*
5. Damson, *Prunus domestica*
6. Dyer's Chamomile, *Anthemis tinctoria*
7. Dyer's Greenweed, *Genista tinctoria*
8. Elder, *Sambucus nigra*
9. Goldenrod, *Solidago canadensis*
10. Hollyhock, *Althaea rosea nigra*
11. Japanese indigo, *polygonum tinctorium*
12. Madder, *Rubia tinctorum*
13. Marigold, *Tagetes erecta*
14. Meadowsweet, *Filipendula ulmaria*
15. Mullein, *Verbascus thapsus*
16. Onion, *Allium*
17. Privet, *Ligustrum ovalifolium*
18. Rhubarb, *Rheum rhabarbarum*
19. Row of plants kept for seed
20. Saffron, *Crocus sativus*
21. St John's Wort, *Hypericum perforatum*
22. Silver birch, *Betula pendula*
23. Soapwort, *Saponaria officinalis*
24. Tansy, *Tanacetum vulgare*
25. Woad, *Isatis tinctoria*
26. Yellow flag, *Iris pseudacorus*

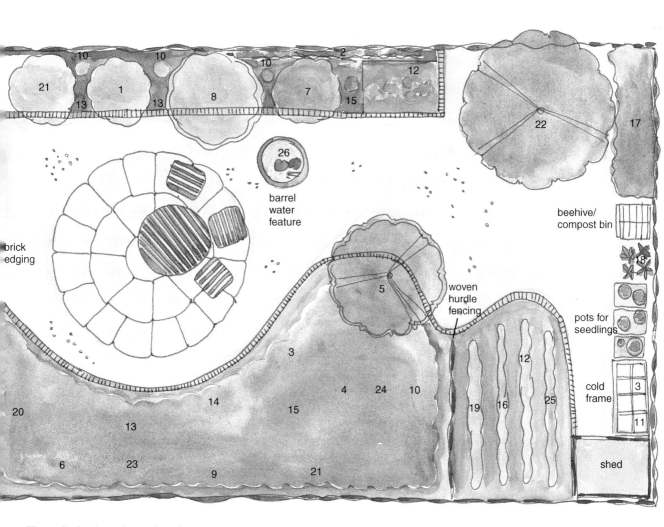

The main dyer's garden – plan view.

The main dyer's garden – axonometric projection.

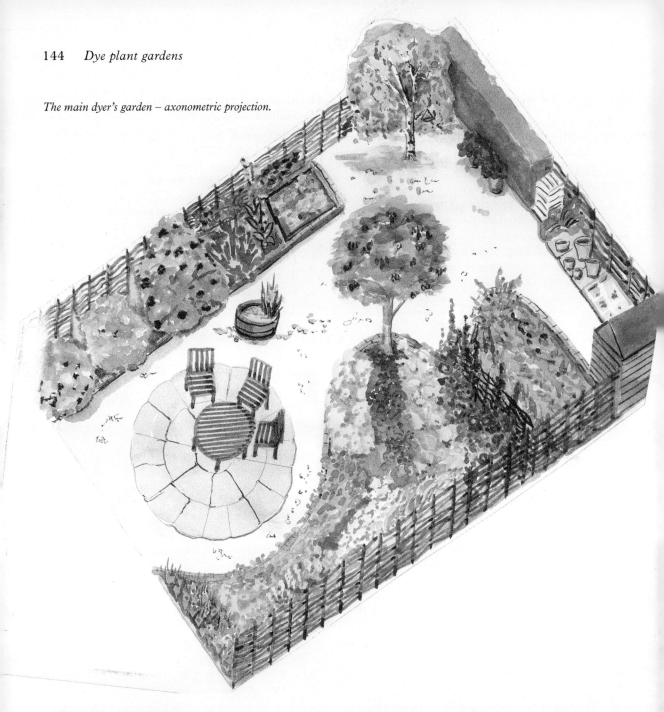

FRONT GARDEN
7.5m × 7.5m (25ft × 25ft)

The front garden lends itself well to dye plants, most of which are hardy. Shrubs and trees can provide both colour and privacy. Weed plants for which you only need the root, may, if you wish, be grown where car wheels run, protected by long-life, heavy duty, cast-iron style rubber matting. Regular rolling will prevent the plants from seeding, but access through the matting will allow the roots to be dug. Be sure the mats are laid on flat sand for durability, and filled with gravel from above to level this bit with the rest of the drive. This design, which is planned for a western aspect also incorporates other functions often required of a front garden, including bin access, bicycle storage, and permeable ground to limit water run-off.

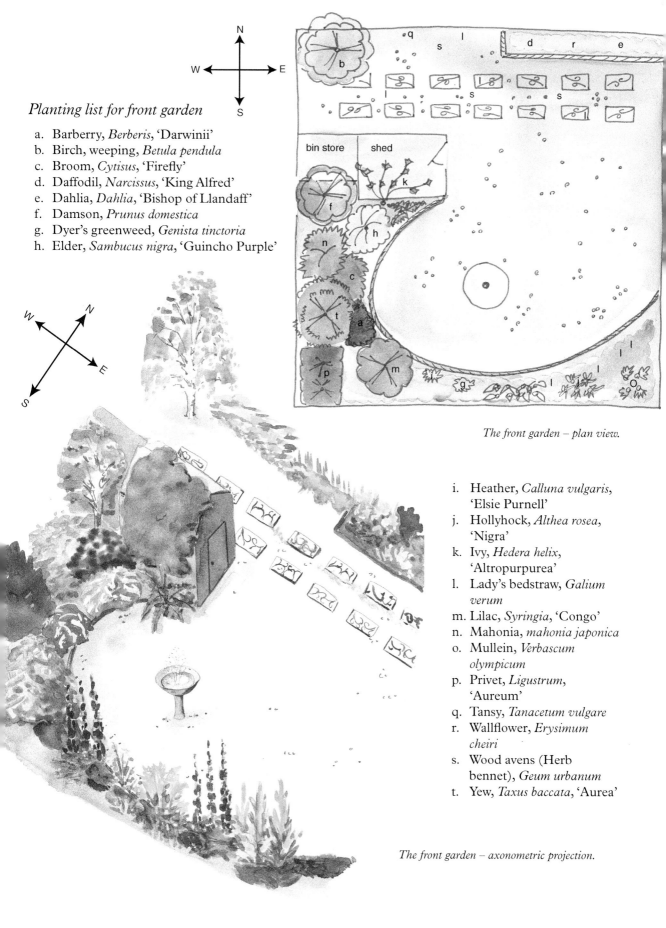

Planting list for front garden

a. Barberry, *Berberis*, 'Darwinii'
b. Birch, weeping, *Betula pendula*
c. Broom, *Cytisus*, 'Firefly'
d. Daffodil, *Narcissus*, 'King Alfred'
e. Dahlia, *Dahlia*, 'Bishop of Llandaff'
f. Damson, *Prunus domestica*
g. Dyer's greenweed, *Genista tinctoria*
h. Elder, *Sambucus nigra*, 'Guincho Purple'

i. Heather, *Calluna vulgaris*, 'Elsie Purnell'
j. Hollyhock, *Althea rosea*, 'Nigra'
k. Ivy, *Hedera helix*, 'Altropurpurea'
l. Lady's bedstraw, *Galium verum*
m. Lilac, *Syringia*, 'Congo'
n. Mahonia, *mahonia japonica*
o. Mullein, *Verbascum olympicum*
p. Privet, *Ligustrum*, 'Aureum'
q. Tansy, *Tanacetum vulgare*
r. Wallflower, *Erysimum cheiri*
s. Wood avens (Herb bennet), *Geum urbanum*
t. Yew, *Taxus baccata*, 'Aurea'

The front garden – plan view.

The front garden – axonometric projection.

WET GARDEN
10.6m × 13.7m (35ft × 45ft)

The wet garden is designed for a north aspect and a heavy clay soil, though the aspect is less important than the drainage. Earth moving will be needed, and professional advice should be taken on the drainage required for your soil type, and the requirement for the pond liner.

Cross sections show the levels of soil that will ensure that some parts of the garden drain well, while others drain into the pond and prevent the wet area from drying out in the summer. Grit and compost can be added and worked into the soil in the beds. Gardens that are naturally very wet can be regulated by planting double the number of trees.

Stepping stones of diminishing size (set below the level of the grass to allow for mowing) serve as a path, and the bed edges are also stone paving. Larger boulders stabilize the soil on the bank and consolidate the wild look set by the rough natural area round the pond where the plants grow tall. The pond will be a haven for wildlife.

The main feature of the garden is the pavilion-style shed with small veranda for deck chairs. The run-off from the shed roof can be used for seasonal adjustment of moisture levels.

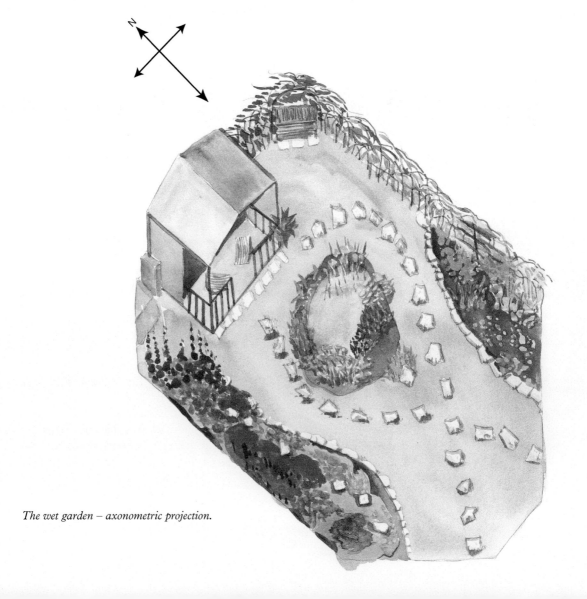

The wet garden – axonometric projection.

Planting list for wet garden

A. Alkanet, *Anchusa tinctoria*
B. Barberry, *Berberis*, 'Rubrostilla'
C. Bistort, *Polygonum bistorta*
D. Blackberry, *Rubus fruticosus*, 'Merton Thornless'
E. Daffodil, *Narcissus pseudonarcissus*
F. Dahlia, *Dahlia*, 'Coltness Gem'
G. Fern, *Dryopteris filix-mas*
H. Goldenrod, *Solidago*, 'Goldenmosa'
I. Gypsywort, *Lycopus europaeus*
J. Hemp agrimony, *Eupatorium cannabinum*

K. Hollyhock, *Althaea rosea*, 'Nigra'
L. Japanese indigo, *Polygonum tinctorium*
M. Marigold, *Tagetes erecta*, 'Cinnabar'
N. Marigold, *Tagetes erecta*, 'Vanilla'
O. Meadowsweet, *Filipendula ulmaria*
P. Rhubarb, *Rheum rhabarbarum*
Q. Soapwort, *Saponaria officinalis*
R. Tansy, *Tanacetum vulgare*
S. Wallflower, *Cheiranthus cheiri*
T. Willow, *Salix viminalis*, 'Osier'
U. Woad, *Isatis tinctoria*
V. Yellow flag iris, *Iris pseudacorus*

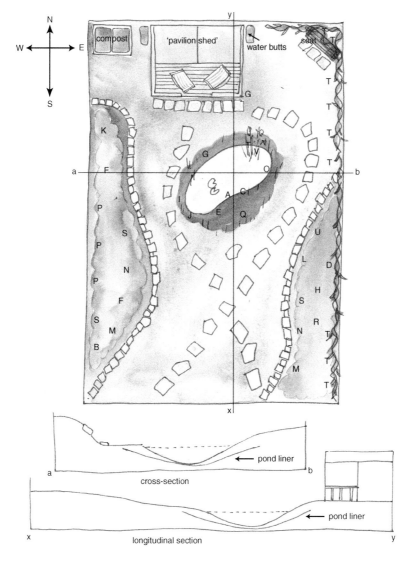

The wet garden – plan view.

DRY GARDEN
10.6m × 13.7m (35ft × 45ft)

The dry garden with a south facing aspect is an opportunity to grow many of the dye plants that flourish on dry and poor soil. Low maintenance also makes it a suitable garden for a larger area where trees can grow unclipped. The irregular-shaped central lawn will offer tantalizing and changing glimpses through the trees and shrubs as they mature. The tree ivy in the shadow of the walnut tree can be cultivated by taking a cutting from the mature upright stems of the fruiting ivy. Keep the Japanese indigo by the water butt for frequent watering and place the rhubarb and woad where they will benefit from the proximity to the compost bins and get direct run-off from the back half of the shed roof.

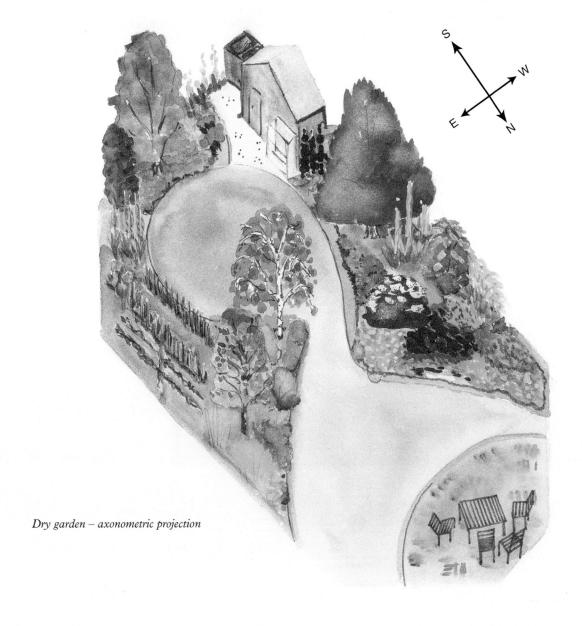

Dry garden – axonometric projection

Planting list for dry garden

1. Birch, *Betula papyrifera*
2. Blackberry, *Rubus fruticosus*, 'Merton Thornless'
3. Broom, *Cytisus scoparius*, Andreannus??
4. Coreopsis, *Calliopsis tinctoria*, 'Sunburst'
5. Daffodil, *Narcissus*, 'King Alfred'
6. Dahlia, *Dahlia*, 'Bishop of Llandaff'
7. Damson, *Prunus domestica*, 'Merryweather'
8. Dyer's Chamomile, *Anthemis tinctoria*
9. Dyer's Greenweed, *Genista tinctoria*
10. Elder, *Sambucus nigra*, 'Guincho purple'
11. Goldenrod, *Solidago*, 'Goldenmosa'
12. Heather, *Calluna vulgaris*, 'Elsie Purnell'
13. Hollyhock, *Althaea rosea*, 'Nigra'
14. Ivy, Tree ivy, *Hedera helix*, 'Arborescens'
15. Japanese indigo, *Polygonum tinctorium*
16. Lady's bedstraw, *Galium verum*
17. Lilac, *Syringa vulgaris*, 'Madame Antoine Buchner'
18. Mahonia, *Mahonia japonica*, 'Napaulensis'
19. Marigold, *Tagetes erecta*, 'Antigua' series
20. Mullein, *Verbascum olympicum*
21. Marjoram, Pot Marjoram, *Origanum marjorana*
22. Onion, *Allium*, 'Red Epicure'
23. Rhubarb, *Rheum rhabarbarum × hybridum*, 'Red Herald'
24. Safflower, *Carthamus tinctorius*
25. St John's Wort, *Hypericum perforatum*
26. Wallflower, *Erysimum cheiri*
27. Walnut, *Juglans nigra*
28. Weld, Dyer's rocket, *Reseda luteola*
29. Woad, *Isatis tinctoria*
30. Yew, *Taxus baccata*, 'Aurea'

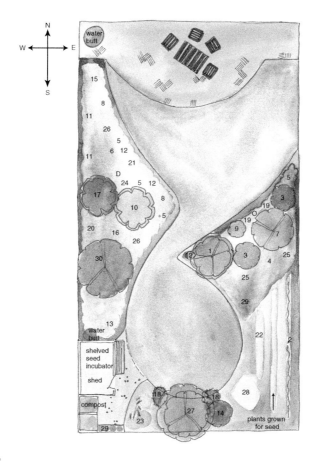

The dry garden – plan view.

CONTAINER GARDEN
6m × 4.5m (20ft × 15ft)

Container growing is ideal for dye plants, many of which can be quite invasive if left to spread. It also gives the opportunity to keep the more delicate ones from being overwhelmed. The plan for this one is to place the containers on a gravel area for drainage. The gravel can either overlay a water-permeable membrane to prevent weed growth, or it can be weed-killed. There is a case for using the latter inorganic method where many robust self-seeding plants are kept in a small space.

The main features of the design structure are:

- the large square fibre refuse bags set within low woven hurdles for the deeper-rooted plants on the ground; and
- the galvanized buckets and watering cans with drainage holes suspended from brackets on strong wire mesh on the vertical boundaries. If they are above standing eye level, they can be set in a shallowly descending line smaller and closer together towards the end of the garden to give a perspective effect of length.

Window boxes set at irregular intervals between pergola posts can comprise a third boundary if the site allows. Fill the containers for heather with ericaceous compost. Install a watering drip feed system along the lines of floor containers and along the line of bucket hooks. The buckets can still be lifted down for repotting and harvesting. A galvanized hipbath is the main water feature overhung by a stunning red variety of rhubarb. Circulating water can flow from a jug in the same raised planting area. Clipped privets (one large and one small) in square metal containers, with the large one nearest the house, will help to give the area the feeling of space, give winter interest, and contrast with the tumble of vegetation in the summer.

A small door at the end of the yard with a mirror 'window' in it will also seem to extend the area. Be sure that the mirror does not reflect the two clipped privets, or the descending line of buckets, or the reverse reflection will neutralize the perspective effect.

Container garden plan

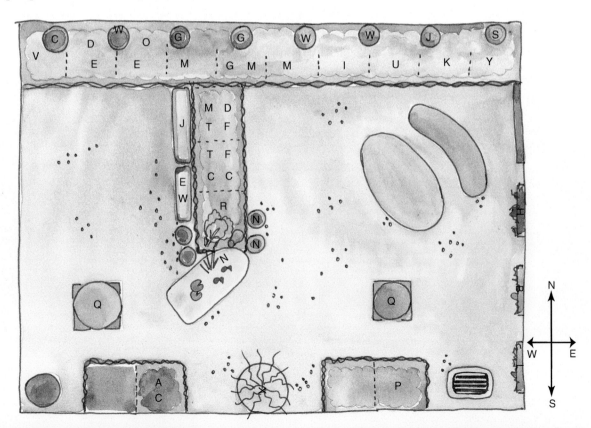

Planting list for container garden

A. Alkanet, *Anchusa tinctoria*
B. Barberry, *Berberis thunbergii*, 'Crimson Pigmy'
C. Bistort, *Polygonum bistorta*
D. Coreopsis, *Calliopsis tinctoria*, 'Limerock Dream'
E. Daffodil, *Narcissus*, 'Ambergate'
F. Dahlia, *Dahlia*, Dwarf cultivar, 'Scarlet Fern'
G. Heather, *Erica × darleyensis*, 'Silberschmelze'
H. Ivy, *Hedera helix*, 'Glacier'
I. Japanese indigo, *Polygonum tinctorium*
J. Lady's bedstraw, *Galium verum*
K. Madder, *Rubia tinctorum*
L. Mahonia, *Mahonia nervosa*
M. Marigold, *Tagetes erecta*, 'Antigua' series

N. Marjoram, *Origanum marjorana*
O. Mullein, *Verbascum olympicum*
P. Onion, *Allium*, 'Red Sun'
Q. Privet, *Ligustrum vulgare*, 'Aureum'
R. Rhubarb, *Rheum × hybridum*, 'Ace of Hearts'
S. Safflower, *Carthamus tinctorius*
T. Saffron, *Crocus sativa*
U. Soapwort, *Saponaria officinalis*
V. Tansy, *Tanacetum vulgare*
W. Wallflower, *Erysimum cheiri*, 'Apricot twist'
X. Willow, *Salix alba*, 'Vitellina'
Y. Woad, *Isatis tinctoria*
Z. Yellow flag iris, *Iris pseudacorus*

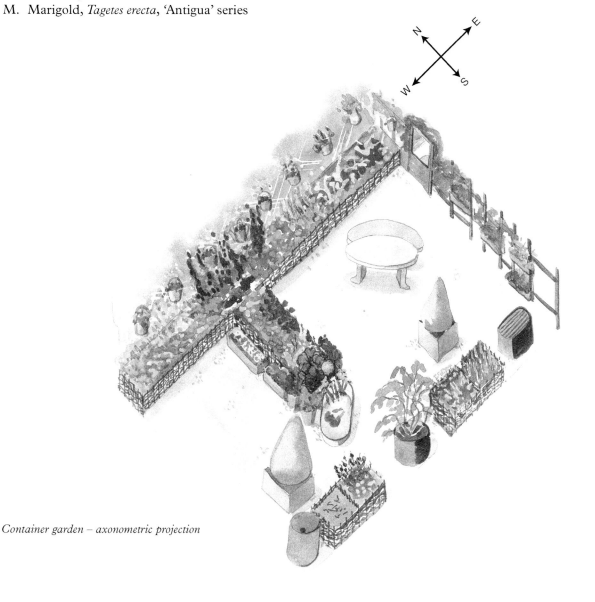

Container garden – axonometric projection

APPENDIX 1

Dye plant index

Agrimony *Agrimonia eupatoria*. Tops: beige to brown. Flowers: yellow.

Alkanet (Dyer's bugloss) *Anchusa tinctoria*. Root bark: (with alcohol) red.

Barberry *Berberis vulgaris*. Bark: (with chrome) brown, (with copper) yellow. Shoots and leaves: gold.

Birch *Betula pendula*. Bark: pink brown. Leaves and catkins: yellow, orange.

Bistort *Polygonum bistorta*. Roots: pinky browns. Leaves: khaki.

Blackberry *Rubus fruticosus*. Berries: pale lilac. Shoots: light green.

Blackthorn *Prunus spinosa*. Blossom: orange. Leaves: greeny yellow. Sloes: pale lilac.

Broom *Cytisus scoparius*. Flowers: yellow. Shoots: green. Bark: yellow-brown.

Coreopsis (Tickseed) *Calliopsis tinctoria*. Flowers: yellow, gold, red-orange, dark brown.

Daffodil *Narcissus pseudonarcissus*. Flowers: (with iron) yellow and green.

Dahlia *Dahlia variabilis*. Flowers: yellows and oranges.

Damson *Prunus domestica*. Fruit: (with tin) dark red. Bark: yellow-brown.

Dandelion *Taraxacum officinalis*. Flowers: green-yellow. Roots: light brown.

Dock *Rumex obtusifolius*. Root: orange, brown, black. Leaves: (with iron) gold and green.

Dyer's chamomile *Anthemis tinctoria*. Flowers and leaves: golden orange. Leaves: yellowy green.

Dyer's greenweed *Genista tinctoria*. Stem and flowers: bright yellow, gold.

Elder *Sambucus nigra*. Berries: pale lilac. Leaves: yellow, orange, khaki.

Fern (Mala fern) *Dryopteris filix-mas*. Leaves: yellow, green, brown.

Goldenrod *Solidago canadensis*. Flowers and stalks: yellow, gold.

Gorse *Ulex europaeus*. Flowers: yellow, orange.

Great Mullein *Verbascum thapsus*. Leaves and stalks: yellow, gold.

Gypsywort *Lycopus europaeus*. Juice: brown, black. Tops: green.

Heather *Calluna vulgaris*. Tops: pinky brown, yellow.

Hemp agrimony *Eupatorium cannabinum*. Tops: yellow, green. Flowers: yellow.

Hollyhock *Alcea rosea*. Black flowers: green. Leaves: lime, pink. Flowers: yellow, orange, tan.

Ivy *Hedera helix*. Leaves: greeny yellow. Berries: grey, green.

Japanese indigo *Polygonum tinctorium*. Leaves and stem: blue.

Lady's bedstraw *Galium verum*. Roots: orangey red.

Lilac *Syringa vulgaris*. Flowers: dull yellow. Leaves: bright yellow.

Madder *Rubia tinctorum*. Roots: pink to Turkey-red.

Mahonia, Oregon grape *Mahonia japonica*. Leaves: yellow green. Stems: gold, green.

Marigold *Tagetes erecta*. Flowers: pale yellow, gold.

Meadowsweet *Filipendula ulmaria*. Tops: greenish yellow. Roots: rose, black.

Nettle *Urtica dioica*. Juice: green. Tops: pale yellow.

Oak *Quercus robur* (mordant). Bark: orange, tan. Leaves: yellow, green.

Onion *Allium*. Red skins: dark tan. Yellow skins: strong gold, yellow.

Perforated St John's wort *Hypericum perforatum*. Flowering tips: pinky brown, and (with acid) red.

Pot Marjoram *Origanum marjorana*. Tops: green. Flowers: old gold.

Privet *Ligustrum vulgare*. Leaves: yellow, gold, (with iron) green.

Ragwort *Senecio jacobaea*. Flowers: yellow, brown. Stems and leaves: green.

Rhubarb *Rheum rhabarbarum* (mordant). Roots: golden yellow.

Safflower *Carthamus tinctorius*. Flowers: yellow, pink.

Saffron *Crocus sativus*. Stigma: yellow.

Soapwort *Saponaria officinalis* (for washing delicate fibres). Flowers: pale green and yellow.

Sorrel *Rumex acetosa* (mordant). Leaves: (with tin) yellow. Roots: yellow and orange.

Tansy *Tanacetum vulgare*. Leaves: yellow, green. Flowers: greenish yellow, orange.

Wallflower *Erysimum cheiri*. Tops: pale green.

Walnut *Juglans nigra*. Leaves: orange, yellow. Husk: brown.

Weld (Dyer's rocket) *Reseda luteola*. Whole plant: vivid yellows, (with woad) Saxon green, Lincoln green.

Willow *Salix*. Bark and twigs: orange, gold. Leaves: yellow, brown.

Woad *Isatis tinctoria* (vat dye). Leaves: blue.

Wood avens (Herb bennet) *Geum urbanum*. Dried root keeps moths away.

Yellow iris (Flag) *Iris pseudacorus*. Flowers: yellow. Rhizomes: pinky brown. Leaves: dark green.

Yew *Taxus baccata*. Fresh heartwood: pink, orange, tan.

Konya kelim dyed with indigo and madder.

APPENDIX 2

Conversion of measurements

The units used in this book are in metric because this is easier to use when calculating the proportions of mordants as percentages needed for a given weight of fibre.

7% of mordant for 500g of yarn
This would be 0.07 × 500 = 35g

or $\dfrac{7}{100}$ × 500 = 35g

or 7g for every 100g so 7 × 5 = 35g

If the weight was say 1 pound (lb) this is
   16 ounces (oz)
0.07 × 16 = 1.12 oz which would be very difficult
   to weigh accurately.

Weights
10 grams (g) = 0.35 oz
1 kilograms (kg) = 1000g = 35.3 oz = 2 lbs 3.3 oz
1 oz = 28.35g
1 lb = 16 oz = 453.6 g

Volumes
1 litre (l) = 1000 millilitres (ml)
          = 1.76 pints (Imperial)
          = 2.13 pints (US)
1 Imperial gallon = 8 pints = 4.546 litres
1 US gallon = 8 US pints = 3.736 litres
1 Imperial pint = 587ml
1 US pint = 467ml
5 ml = 1 teaspoon
15ml = 1 tablespoon
30ml = 1 fluid ounce

Temperatures
Celsius (Centigrade) ranges from 0° C freezing to
   100° C boiling
Fahrenheit ranges from 32° F freezing to 212° F
   boiling

$$°F = \frac{9 \times °C}{5} + 32 \quad \text{and} \quad °C = \frac{5(°F - 32)}{9}$$

To convert from Celsius to Fahrenheit: take the
   °C multiply by 9, divide by 5 and add 32.
To convert from Fahrenheit to Celsius: take the
   °F subtract 32, multiply by 5 and divide by 9.

Heights
10 centimetres (cm) = 3.9 inches (in)
1metre (m) = 100cm = 39.4 in

1 in = 2.54 cm
1 foot (ft) = 12 in = 30.46 cm

Glossary

Acetic acid Household vinegar has 5% acetic acid, used to alter pH in rinse water for berry dyes.

Additive dye A dye that needs a mordant to adhere to the fibre.

Adjective dye A dye that needs a mordant to adhere to the fibre.

After-mordant A mordant such as copper or chrome to improve fastness and darken the colour. This means that once the initial dyeing process is completed, then the yarn is put into the second mordant bath, brought to the simmer in 30 minutes and kept at that temperature for a further 30 minutes, then removed and rinsed.

Alum Aluminium potassium sulphate, mordant, used with cream of tartar as an assistant.

Ammonia Household ammonia used to alter pH in rinse for berry dyes.

Annual A plant that grows for only one season.

Assistant A chemical that improves the uptake of a mordant, reducing the quantity needed.

Batts Carded fibre in sheets of parallel fibres, which are as wide as the carding machine rollers and can be a metre or more in width and 4cm in depth.

Biennial A plant that produces a rosette in the first year and a flower spike in its second and final year.

Bleeding When colour is washed out after the dye process.

Blooming To brighten the colour by adding a tin mordant.

Bottoming *See* top dyeing.

Chrome Potassium dichromate, mordant that must be kept in a dark jar and is poisonous, used with formic acid as an assistant.

Cold frame A glass or plastic low structure used to protect young plants from cold and adverse weather.

Cold stratification Putting seeds in a plastic bag with slightly moistened paper towel in the refrigerator for from one to three months before planting out; this simulates natural conditions.

Compost Decayed vegetable matter used to improve soil structure.

Common salt Sodium chloride added to rinse reduces bleeding of colour.

Copper Copper sulphate, mordant used with formic acid as an assistant.

Cream of tartar Potassium hydrogen tartrate, assistant to alum. Baking powder can be used, but may contain sodium pyrophosphate instead of cream of tartar, which is not as effective.

Deciduous A tree that sheds its leaves at the end of the growing season.

Direct dye A dye that does not require a mordant, but tends to be fugitive.

Dye bath A solution of dyestuff either with the plant matter still in or as a liquor with it removed.

Exhaust Dye liquor after the initial dye process when there is still some colour remaining so produces a lighter shade.

Extract Result of removing the colour element of the dye plant by boiling, squeezing or soaking.

Fast When the colour remains the same after being exposed to light, washing and the air.

Felt Woollen fibres shrunk and matted together by changing from hot to cold and by rubbing.

Formic acid Assistant to chrome mordant, produces an unpleasant smell when used.

Fugitive A colour that is initially bright, which fades on exposure to light and washing.

Glaubers salts Sodium sulphate, used as a levelling agent.

Hank A skein of yarn, loosely tied in several places, ready for dyeing.

Herbaceous A plant having a soft stem rather than a woody one.

Husk The outer covering of a fruit such as walnut.

Indigotin The active ingredient of woad and indigo.

Iron Ferrous sulphate, used to sadden colours but tends to rot wool.

Kemp Hollow brittle fibre, which does not take the dye.

Lanolin Natural grease secreted by sheep to protect the fleece, needs to be removed before dyeing.

Levelling agent Chemical that disperses evenly throughout the fibre such as Glaubers salts.

Loft This is when the felt retains more spring because the crimps in the fibre have not been straightened out by industrial scouring and the mechanical felting process using heavy rollers or plates.

Mordant Chemical that fixes the dye to the fibre and improves the wash and light fastness.

Mordanting The process that prepares the fibre to accept the dye pigment.

Natural dye Dyestuffs found in parts of plants such as flowers, fruits and roots.

Over dyeing *See* top dyeing.

Oxalic acid Used as a mordant, contained in rhubarb leaves and sorrel. Assistant to tin mordant.

Oxidize In indigo dyeing, the addition of oxygen to the indigo molecules changing the colour of the fibre from yellow to blue.

Perennial A plant that lives more than two years.

pH Measure of acidity or alkalinity on the scale of 1 (most acidic) to 14 (most alkaline). pH 7 is neutral.

Reducing agent A chemical that removes oxygen, as needed in the indigo process.

Rhizome An underground rootlike stem, bearing both roots and shoots.

Roving Carded fibre in a neat coil without a twist.

Saddening To make a colour duller by adding iron.

Saporins The naturally occurring soaps such as in Soapwort.

Scouring Removing grease from wool by washing in soap.

Skein A wool winding usually tied loosely in a figure of eight to retain order of strands.

Sliver Carded fibre in a neat coil without a twist.

Solution A mixture of a liquid and a dissolved chemical.

Stigma Part of a flower that collects pollen.

Substantive dye A dye that is deposited on the surface of the fibre, such as indigo.

Swift A yarn winder.

Tannin Can be used as a mordant, found in tree bark but mainly used to tan leather. Used as mordant for cotton.

Tin Stannous chloride, a mordant, poisonous and brightens the colour but can make fibre brittle; oxalic acid used as an assistant.

Top dyeing When dye is used once another colour has been applied.

Tops A continuous woollen roving.

Vat dye A substantive dye where the dye is on the surface of the fibre such as indigo.

Washing soda Sodium carbonate, a strong alkali used in cleaning fibres and in the indigo process.

Yolk A layer of grease found in raw fleece marking the point at which the fleece growth slowed in winter. This needs to be washed out before the dyeing process.

Suppliers

DRIED DYE PLANTS AND MORDANTS, BOOKS, FIBRES AND EQUIPMENT

British Wool Marketing Board, Woolhouse, Roydsdale Way, Euroway Trading Estate, Bradford, BD4 6SE
www.britishwool.org.uk (fleece from named breeds)

Chiltern Seeds, Bortree Stile, Ulverston, Cumbria LA12 7PB
www.chilternseeds.co.uk
01229 584549 (dye plant seeds)

Dharma Trading Co., PO Box 150916, San Rafael, California, 9491, USA
www.dharmatrading.com

Earth Guild, 33 Haywood Street, Asheville, North Carolina, 28801, USA
www.earthguild.com
828 255 7818

Fibrecrafts, Old Portsmouth Road, Peasmarsh, Guildford, GU7 2QD
www.fibrecrafts.com
01483 565800 (dye plants, mordants, books, equipment)

Frank Herring, 27 High West Street, Dorchester, Dorset DT1 1UP
01305 264449 (dyes, mordants, fibre, equipment)
info@frankherringandsons.com

Handweavers Studio, 29 Haroldstone Road, London, E17 7AN
www.handweaversstudio.co.uk
020 8521 2281 (dye plants, mordants, books)

Kevock Garden Plants, 16 Kevock Road, Lasswade, Midlothian, EH18 1HT
www.kevockgarden.co.uk
0131 454 0660 (saffron crocus bulbs)

PM Woolcraft, Pindon End, Hanslope, Milton Keynes, MK19 7HN
www.naturaldyes.co.uk
01908 510277 (dye plants, mordants, books, equipment)

Sandy Mush Herb Nursery, Rt 2 Surrett Cove Road, Leicester, North Carolina, 28748, USA
www.sandymushherbs
828 683 2014

Suffolk Herbs, Monks Farm, Coggeshall, Kelvedon, Essex CO5 9PG
www.suffolkherbs.com
01376 572456 (dye plant seeds)

The Woolery, PO Box 468, Murfeeboro, North Carolina, 27855, USA
www.woolery.com
252 398 4581

Wingham Wool Fibre Merchants, Old Building Yard, Wentworth, Rotherham, South Yorkshire (Mordants, fibres and equipment)
www.winghamwoolwork.co.uk

Bibliography

Adrosko, Rita J., *Natural Dyes and Home Dyeing* (Dover Publications 1971)

Balfour-Paul, Jenny, *Indigo* (British Museum Press 1998)

Barber, Elizabeth, *Women's work, The first 20,000 Years* (W.W.Norton & Co 1994)

Bohmer, Harald, *Koekboya, Natural Dyes and Textiles: a colour journey from Turkey to India and beyond* (REMHOB- Verlag 2002)

Buchanan, Rita, *Weaver's Garden* (Interweave Press 1987)

Burkett, Mary E., *The Art of the Feltmaker* (Titus Wilson and Son Ltd, Kendal 1979)

Cardon, Dominique, *Le Monde de Teinture Naturel* (Belin 2003)

Dalby, Gill, *Natural Dyes, Fast and Fugitive* (Ashill Publications 1992)

Dalby, Gill, & Christmas, Liz, *Spinning and Dyeing* (David and Charles)

Duke, Dee, & Edlin White, Rowena *A Calendar of Common Dye Plants No 10* (Woolgatherings for dyers and spinners)

Edmonds, John, *History of Woad and the Medieval Woad Vat, no1* (1998)

Edmonds, John, *The History and Practice of Eighteenth Century Dyeing, no 2* (1999)

Edmonds, John, *Medieval Textile Dyeing, no3* (2003)

Fowler, Brenda, *Iceman* (Pan Macmillan Ltd 2002)

Mabey, Richard, *Plants with a Purpose* (Collins 1977)

Murphy, Brian, *The Root of Wild Madder* (Simon and Schuster Paperbacks 2005)

Royal Horticultural Society Journal, *The Garden* (www.rhs.org.uk)

Schetky, E McD., *Brooklyn Botanic Garden Record Vol 20 No3.*

Simmons, Jenni, *A Shetland Dye Book* (The Shetland Times 1985)

Sjoberg, Gunilla Paetam, *New Directions for Felt: an ancient craft* (Interweave Press 1996)

Stapley, Christina, *Herbcraft Naturally* (Heartsease Books 1994)

Thurston, Violetta, *The Use of Vegetable Dyes* (Dryad Press 1949)

Index